THE ESSENTIAL LONG-TERM WILDERNESS SURVIVAL BIBLE

7 in 1 Forge Your Path to Independence with Expert Techniques for Navigating and Thriving in the Untamed Wilderness

Brenner Whitt

TABLE OF CONTENTS

BOOK 1: THE ESSENTIALS OF SURVIVAL

1. SURVIVAL MINDSET

1.1 UNDERSTANDING STRESS AND PANIC

Understanding stress and panic in survival situations is fundamental to maintaining a clear head and ensuring your actions are purposeful and effective. The wilderness, with its unpredictable elements and isolation, can be a breeding ground for anxiety. Yet, recognizing these emotional responses and managing them effectively is a critical survival skill.

When thrust into a survival scenario, your body undergoes a series of physiological changes designed to prepare you for fight or flight. This stress response is an ancient mechanism that has enabled humans to react swiftly to threats. Your heart rate increases, pumping more blood to your muscles, your breathing quickens to supply more oxygen, and your senses become heightened. However, while these changes are beneficial in the short term, prolonged stress can impair your judgment and deplete your energy reserves.

One of the first steps in managing stress is understanding its origins. In the wild, stress can arise from various sources: fear of the unknown, the physical challenge of survival tasks, and the pressure to protect oneself and possibly others. Recognizing these triggers is crucial because it allows you to address the root cause rather than just the symptoms. For example, if you fear getting lost, equipping yourself with better navigation skills can alleviate this anxiety.

A practical way to mitigate stress is through preparation and knowledge. The more you know about the environment and the survival techniques you'll need, the more confident you'll feel. This confidence can significantly reduce the initial shock and panic that often accompany unexpected situations. Take the time to learn and practice essential skills like fire-starting, shelter-building, and water purification. Rehearsing these skills under non-stressful conditions builds muscle memory, making them easier to execute when you're under duress.

Equally important is the mental preparation. Visualization is a powerful tool used by athletes and survivalists alike. By mentally rehearsing survival scenarios and visualizing successful outcomes, you can train your mind to respond calmly and effectively when reality strikes. This mental conditioning can create a sense of familiarity, reducing the shock factor when you find yourself in an actual survival situation.

In the wilderness, maintaining a routine can also be a powerful stress reliever. Structure your day with specific tasks and goals. Not only does this keep you busy, but it also provides a sense of normalcy and control. Even simple routines, like setting up and breaking down camp, can provide comfort and predictability. Remember, your mindset can be as much of a tool as your physical equipment. A disciplined mind can help you stay focused, conserve energy, and make sound decisions.

Another key aspect of managing stress is staying in the moment. It's easy to become overwhelmed by the enormity of a survival situation, but dwelling on worst-case scenarios can paralyze you with fear. Instead, focus on immediate, manageable tasks. Break down your situation into smaller, actionable steps. For example, if you're lost, your immediate goal might be to find a safe place to camp for the night. Once that's achieved, you can then focus on signaling for help or finding your way out. This approach not only makes the situation less daunting but also helps you feel a sense of accomplishment as you achieve each small goal.

Panic, on the other hand, is an intense and immediate reaction to a perceived threat. It can cause you to act irrationally, make poor decisions, or freeze up entirely. Recognizing the onset of panic and having strategies to combat it are essential.

One effective technique is controlled breathing. When you feel panic setting in, take slow, deep breaths. This simple act can help slow your heart rate and bring your body back to a more manageable state. Inhale deeply through your nose, hold the breath for a few seconds, and then exhale slowly through your mouth. Repeat this process several times until you feel your body begin to calm down.

Talking to yourself might seem odd, but it's a proven method to regain control. Positive self-talk can interrupt the cycle of panic and reframe your mindset. Remind yourself of your skills, your plan, and the steps you need to take next. Phrases like "I can handle this" or "Stay calm and think clearly" can reinforce a sense of control and competence.

Connecting with the environment rather than seeing it as an adversary can also help. Observing the natural world—listening to the birds, feeling the wind, watching the trees—can ground you and reduce feelings of isolation and fear. This connection can transform your surroundings from a source of threat to a partner in your survival. Embrace the rhythms of nature and use them to your advantage.

Physical health is closely tied to mental health. Ensure you're taking care of your body by staying hydrated, eating when possible, and getting rest. Physical exhaustion can exacerbate feelings of stress and panic, making it harder to think clearly and make rational decisions. Even in survival situations, try to find moments to rest and recuperate. Your body and mind are your most valuable assets, and maintaining them is crucial. Lastly, never underestimate the power of hope and positivity. Survival stories often highlight individuals who endured extreme conditions through sheer willpower and a positive outlook. Hope can be a powerful motivator, giving you the strength to push through the hardest moments. Cultivate an attitude of resilience and adaptability. Accept that challenges will arise and that you have the capability to overcome them. Every challenge faced and surmounted in the wilderness is a testament to your strength and resourcefulness.

1.2 BUILDING MENTAL RESILIENCE

Building mental resilience in the wilderness is akin to forging steel—under the right conditions, it becomes stronger and more enduring. Survival isn't just about the physical acts of finding water, food, and shelter; it's deeply rooted in the mind's ability to adapt, endure, and overcome. Mental resilience is the backbone of survival, enabling you to face the unknown with confidence and courage.

Mental resilience begins with acceptance. The wilderness is an unpredictable, often harsh environment, and accepting this reality is the first step towards mental fortitude. Resistance to this truth only breeds frustration and fear. By acknowledging that the wilderness will challenge you in ways you can't always anticipate, you prepare your mind to adapt and find solutions. Acceptance doesn't mean giving up; it means recognizing the situation for what it is and moving forward with a clear head.

One of the most powerful tools in building resilience is maintaining a positive outlook. Positivity might seem like a luxury in dire circumstances, but it's a crucial element of survival. Optimism fuels hope, and hope can drive you to keep pushing when your body and mind are exhausted. Reflect on past challenges you've overcome and remind yourself of your capabilities. Each small victory, no matter how insignificant it may seem, is a building block for resilience. Whether it's successfully starting a fire or navigating a difficult terrain, these moments affirm your ability to survive.

Visualization is another technique that can fortify your mental resilience. Athletes and survivalists alike use this method to mentally prepare for challenging situations. Visualize yourself successfully completing survival tasks, from building a shelter to foraging for food. Picture every detail—the sounds, the smells, the tactile sensations. This mental rehearsal builds familiarity, reducing the anxiety that comes with the unknown. When the time comes to perform these tasks in real life, your mind will have a blueprint to follow, making the process less daunting and more manageable.

Routine can also be a sanctuary for the mind in chaotic environments. Establishing a daily routine, even in the wilderness, provides a sense of normalcy and control. It's about finding small anchors in a sea of uncertainty. Wake up at the same time each day, plan your tasks, and stick to a schedule as much as possible. This structure helps to ground you, providing a framework within which you can operate effectively.

Mindfulness, the practice of staying present in the moment, is another pillar of mental resilience. In survival situations, it's easy to become overwhelmed by the magnitude of the challenges ahead. Mindfulness helps to focus your attention on the here and now, breaking down overwhelming tasks into manageable steps. Pay attention to your surroundings—the rustle of leaves, the flow of a stream, the feel of the earth beneath your feet. This connection with your environment can calm your mind and sharpen your senses, making you more attuned to potential resources and dangers.

Building mental resilience also involves embracing adaptability. The wilderness is dynamic, and conditions can change rapidly. Flexibility in your approach allows you to respond to these changes without panic. This adaptability isn't just about physical actions but also about shifting your mindset. If one method of achieving a goal fails, don't dwell on the setback. Instead, reassess the situation and consider alternative strategies. Every obstacle is an opportunity to learn and grow, enhancing your overall resilience.

Another critical aspect of mental resilience is self-compassion. It's easy to be hard on yourself when things go wrong, but self-criticism can erode your confidence and resolve. Instead, practice self-compassion. Understand that mistakes are part of the learning process. Forgive yourself, learn from the experience, and move forward. This compassionate approach builds a resilient mindset, where setbacks are seen not as failures but as valuable lessons.

Connection with others, even in solitary survival situations, plays a role in mental resilience. If you're with a group, fostering a sense of camaraderie and mutual support can be immensely beneficial. Share your experiences, listen to others, and provide encouragement. In solitary situations, draw strength from thoughts of loved ones or the broader human experience of survival. Knowing that others have faced and overcome similar challenges can provide a powerful sense of solidarity and motivation.

Maintaining physical health is intrinsically linked to mental resilience. Regular physical exercise, even in minimal forms, can boost your mood and energy levels. Simple exercises, such as stretching or short walks, can keep your body in better shape, which in turn supports a stronger mental state. Proper nutrition and hydration are also vital. Dehydration and malnutrition can impair cognitive function and mood, making it harder to stay mentally resilient. Prioritize finding clean water and nutritious food sources to keep both your body and mind in peak condition.

Lastly, never underestimate the power of rest and recovery. In survival situations, the urge to keep moving and doing can be overwhelming, but burnout is a real threat. Ensure you allocate time for rest. Sleep is a critical component of mental resilience, allowing your mind and body to recover and rejuvenate. Find safe, secure places to rest and try to establish a regular sleep pattern. This rest will not only restore your physical strength but also clear your mind, making you better equipped to handle the challenges ahead.

1.3 STRATEGIC THINKING AND PROBLEM SOLVING

Strategic thinking and problem solving are the twin pillars that support a robust survival mindset. When faced with the unpredictability of the wilderness, your ability to think strategically and solve problems effectively can mean the difference between life and death. These skills help you navigate challenges with a clear head, making informed decisions that enhance your chances of survival.

Strategic thinking begins with situational awareness. This is about understanding your environment and the variables at play. In the wilderness, everything from the weather to the terrain and available resources impacts your strategy. It starts with observation—taking in your surroundings, noting landmarks, potential hazards, and resources. This kind of detailed awareness lays the groundwork for all strategic decisions. For example, noticing the position of the sun can help you determine direction, while identifying water sources can guide your route planning.

A critical aspect of strategic thinking is setting priorities. Not all tasks in a survival situation are of equal importance, and your first job is to identify which are crucial for immediate survival. Typically, this involves securing shelter, water, fire, and food, in that order. But these priorities can shift based on your specific circumstances.

If you're in a cold environment, building a fire might leap to the top of your list to prevent hypothermia. By assessing your situation and setting clear priorities, you ensure that your efforts are focused on the most pressing needs.

Once you've established your priorities, you need to develop a plan of action. This involves breaking down larger goals into manageable steps. Suppose your immediate goal is to build a shelter. Your plan might include selecting a suitable location, gathering materials, and constructing the shelter. Each step should be clear and achievable, reducing the likelihood of feeling overwhelmed by the task at hand. Planning in this way provides a roadmap, allowing you to move forward methodically and with purpose.

However, even the best-laid plans can go awry, which is where problem-solving comes into play. Effective problem-solving starts with a calm and analytical approach. Panic clouds judgment and can lead to hasty decisions, so the first step in addressing any problem is to stay calm. Take a moment to breathe and clear your mind before assessing the situation. This mental reset can make a significant difference in how you perceive and tackle the problem.

Identifying the problem is the next crucial step. This might seem straightforward, but in the wilderness, problems can be complex and multifaceted. For example, if you're unable to start a fire, the issue could be damp materials, lack of proper technique, or even unsuitable conditions. By pinpointing the exact cause, you can address the root of the problem rather than just treating the symptoms. This requires a methodical approach: observe the situation, gather information, and then analyze it to identify the core issue.

Once you have a clear understanding of the problem, brainstorming solutions is the next phase. Creativity is a valuable asset in survival situations. Often, you'll need to think outside the box and use available resources in unconventional ways. For instance, if your fire-starting materials are damp, you might need to find a way to dry them out, such as placing them in a sunny spot or near your body for warmth. This creative problem-solving mindset enables you to adapt and overcome obstacles using the resources at hand.

After generating potential solutions, evaluate each one for feasibility and potential outcomes. Consider the risks and benefits of each option. This is where strategic thinking and problem-solving intersect; you're using your analytical skills to weigh options and choose the most effective path forward. Sometimes, the best solution isn't the most obvious one, but rather the one that balances immediate needs with long-term survival.

Decision-making in the wilderness often requires a balance between speed and deliberation. While some situations demand quick action, others benefit from careful consideration. Knowing when to act swiftly and when to take your time is a skill that improves with experience and mindfulness. Trust your instincts, but also rely on your knowledge and observations to guide you. Experience is a great teacher, and each decision you make adds to your understanding and competence in survival situations.

Adaptability is another cornerstone of effective problem-solving. The wilderness is ever-changing, and rigid plans can quickly become obsolete. Being flexible allows you to pivot and adjust your strategies as conditions evolve. For example, if a planned route becomes impassable due to flooding, an adaptable mindset enables you to find an alternative path without losing momentum. This adaptability is not just about changing plans, but also about maintaining a positive and proactive attitude in the face of setbacks.

Learning from past experiences is vital for honing your strategic thinking and problem-solving skills. Each challenge you face is an opportunity to grow and improve. Reflect on what worked and what didn't, and use these insights to refine your approach. Keeping a journal can be incredibly helpful, allowing you to track your decisions and their outcomes. Over time, this practice builds a repository of knowledge that enhances your overall survival skills.

Moreover, effective communication, if you are in a group, plays a significant role in strategic thinking and problem-solving. Sharing ideas, observations, and solutions can lead to better outcomes. Collaborative problem-solving often yields creative solutions that might not occur to an individual working alone. In situations where you're alone, communicating with yourself through mental rehearsals or even talking out loud can help clarify your thoughts and solidify your strategies. Maintain a proactive mindset. Rather than waiting for problems to arise, anticipate potential challenges and plan accordingly. This foresight can help you avoid many issues altogether. For instance, if you know a storm is approaching, securing your shelter and gathering extra firewood in advance can save you from scrambling in adverse conditions. Proactivity stems from a combination of knowledge, experience, and an alert mindset, ensuring that you're always a step ahead.

2. Basic Survival Skills

2.1 Finding and Purifying Water

Water is the essence of life, and in the wilderness, securing a reliable source of water is one of the most critical survival tasks. Finding and purifying water is not just about quenching your thirst but ensuring that the water you consume is safe and will sustain you over the long haul. This process requires knowledge, resourcefulness, and sometimes, a bit of ingenuity.

When you're in the wild, the first step in finding water is to understand the landscape. Different terrains offer different clues about where water might be found. In arid regions, for example, water is scarce and often hidden, while in lush, forested areas, it might be more abundant but not necessarily safe to drink without treatment. Observing the natural indicators around you can lead you to water sources. Birds and animals are often excellent guides. Birds tend to congregate around water in the mornings and evenings, and game trails often lead to water sources. Following these trails can be a fruitful strategy. The sound of running water is another clear indicator. Streams and rivers not only provide a more consistent source of water but also tend to be easier to purify. Even in dry areas, you might find water by searching in low-lying areas or depressions where rainwater can accumulate. Rocky outcrops can also be useful; sometimes water can be found in crevices or pooled in natural basins. Early morning dew is another potential source, which can be collected from leaves and grasses using a cloth.

However, finding water is only half the battle. The next crucial step is ensuring that the water is safe to drink. Natural water sources can be contaminated with pathogens, chemicals, and other harmful substances that can cause severe illness. Purifying water involves removing these contaminants to make it safe for consumption.

One of the most reliable methods of purifying water is boiling. Boiling water for at least one minute (or three minutes at higher altitudes) kills most harmful organisms, including bacteria, viruses, and parasites. If you have the means to start a fire and a suitable container, boiling should be your go-to method. However, fire and containers aren't always available, so it's essential to know alternative methods.

Filtering water is another effective way to make it safe. Commercial filters are highly effective, but if you don't have one, you can make a rudimentary filter using natural materials. A basic filter can be made using layers of sand, charcoal, and small rocks. While this won't remove all pathogens, it can significantly reduce particulates and some contaminants. This method is often used in conjunction with boiling for added safety.

Chemical purification is also a viable option. Water purification tablets, which typically contain iodine or chlorine, are lightweight and easy to carry. These tablets are very effective at killing bacteria and viruses, though they require some time to work, often around 30 minutes. It's also essential to follow the instructions carefully to avoid any potential health risks from improper use.

Solar water disinfection (SODIS) is a method that utilizes the sun's ultraviolet rays to purify water. This technique involves filling a clear plastic bottle with water and exposing it to direct sunlight for at least six hours. The UV rays from the sun kill harmful microorganisms, making the water safe to drink. This method is particularly useful in areas with ample sunlight but requires clear plastic bottles, which might not always be available. Foraging for water isn't always about finding a flowing stream or a clear pond. Sometimes, you might need to get creative.

Collecting rainwater is one of the safest ways to secure clean water. Use any available containers or create makeshift funnels with large leaves or tarps to direct rainwater into containers. Remember to boil or filter it if you're unsure about contaminants it might have picked up along the way. In desperate situations, plants can provide water. Certain plants, like cacti, store water in their tissues, though some can be toxic, so proper identification is crucial. Additionally, tree roots can sometimes be tapped for water, and some vines in tropical regions can yield drinkable water when cut.

It's important to note that not all natural water sources are equal. Stagnant water, especially in swamps and bogs, is more likely to be contaminated than flowing water. Always opt for moving water if you have the choice. The clearer the water, the better, but clarity alone doesn't guarantee safety.

Staying hydrated is crucial, but it's equally important to manage your water intake efficiently. Avoid drinking large quantities at once; instead, sip small amounts regularly. This helps your body absorb water more efficiently and reduces the risk of overhydration, which can be as dangerous as dehydration.

2.2 BUILDING A SHELTER

In the wilderness, building a shelter is paramount for survival. It provides protection from the elements, conserves body heat, and offers a psychological comfort that can boost your morale. A well-constructed shelter can make the difference between a miserable night and a restful one, allowing you to face the challenges of the next day with renewed strength and focus.

The first step in building a shelter is choosing the right location. This decision is crucial and involves several factors. You need a spot that offers natural protection from the wind and is safe from potential hazards like falling branches or flash floods. Avoid areas near water sources to reduce the risk of insects and wildlife encounters, but stay within a reasonable distance to ensure you have access to water. Look for a flat area with enough natural materials nearby for constructing your shelter.

Once you've selected a location, it's time to decide on the type of shelter. The environment, available materials, and the duration of your stay will influence this decision. For short-term needs, a simple lean-to or debris hut may suffice, while long-term survival might require a more robust structure like a log cabin. A lean-to shelter is one of the simplest and quickest to build. Start by finding a sturdy, horizontal support beam—this could be a fallen tree or a large branch between two trees. Lean smaller branches against this beam at an angle to create a frame. Cover the frame with leaves, grass, and other insulating materials to protect against wind and rain. For added warmth and wind protection, build a reflector wall of logs or stones on the open side of the lean-to, and if possible, position your fire between the shelter and the reflector wall.

The debris hut is another effective option, particularly in colder climates where insulation is critical. Begin by creating a ridgepole—a sturdy branch propped up on one end by a forked stick or tree. Lean smaller branches against both sides of the ridgepole to form a triangular structure. Pile on leaves, grass, and other insulating materials until the structure is well covered. The thicker the layer, the better the insulation. Leave a small entrance, and if possible, create a door using a piece of bark or additional branches to keep the warmth in and the cold out.

For those planning to stay in one location for an extended period, a more durable shelter like a log cabin may be necessary. This type of shelter requires considerable time and effort but offers superior protection and comfort. Begin by selecting straight, sturdy logs for the walls. Notch the ends of the logs so they fit snugly together at the corners. Stack the logs to your desired height, and fill any gaps with moss, clay, or mud for insulation. The roof can be made from smaller logs, branches, and thatch, creating a waterproof and insulated barrier.

Regardless of the type of shelter, insulation is key. In the wild, the ground can sap your body heat quickly. Use leaves, grass, and pine needles to create a thick bedding layer. This not only insulates you from the cold ground but also provides a more comfortable sleeping surface. If the ground is damp, elevate your bed using logs or rocks to keep dry.

A shelter is not just about physical protection; it also offers psychological benefits. In survival situations, maintaining a positive mental state is crucial. A well-built shelter can provide a sense of security and control, crucial for mental well-being. Take the time to make your shelter as comfortable as possible. Small touches, like a well-organized interior or a fire pit nearby, can make a significant difference in your overall morale. When building a shelter, always be mindful of the Leave No Trace principles. While survival may necessitate using natural resources, try to minimize your impact on the environment. Avoid cutting live trees if possible, and use fallen branches and other natural debris instead. When you leave, dismantle your shelter and scatter the materials to allow the area to return to its natural state.

In addition to physical construction, pay attention to ventilation and drainage. A shelter that's too airtight can lead to condensation and dampness, which can be uncomfortable and unhealthy. Ensure there's adequate airflow to keep the interior dry. Likewise, if it rains, your shelter should have proper drainage to prevent water from pooling inside. A slight slope in the floor or a small trench around the shelter can help direct water away.

Lighting a fire near your shelter provides warmth and a means to cook food, but it must be done safely. Position the fire far enough from the shelter to prevent accidental fires but close enough to benefit from the heat. Use rocks or a fire ring to contain the flames, and always have water or soil nearby to extinguish the fire if necessary.

In all your efforts, remain adaptable. The wilderness is unpredictable, and conditions can change rapidly. Be prepared to modify your shelter or even move if your initial location proves unsuitable. Flexibility and creativity are your allies in survival. What works in one situation may not work in another, so continuously assess your needs and surroundings. Building a shelter is as much an art as it is a skill. It requires an understanding of the environment, resourcefulness, and a keen eye for detail. Each shelter you build enhances your knowledge and proficiency, making you better prepared for future challenges. Whether it's a simple lean-to for a night or a log cabin for an extended stay, your shelter is your sanctuary—a place of safety and rest in the heart of the wilderness.

2.3 SIGNALING FOR HELP

In the wilderness, signaling for help is a vital skill that can make the difference between rescue and prolonged isolation. While self-reliance and survival skills are essential, knowing how to effectively communicate your need for assistance can expedite your return to safety. Signaling methods vary depending on the resources available, the environment, and the situation's urgency, but the key is to make your presence known as clearly and unmistakably as possible.

One of the most universal distress signals is fire. Fire not only provides warmth and a means to cook but also serves as a powerful signal visible from great distances, especially at night. To maximize visibility, build a signal fire in a clearing where it can be seen from the air. Create three fires in a triangular formation or in a straight line, as this configuration is recognized internationally as a distress signal. During the day, add green vegetation or damp materials to create smoke, which is more visible against the sky. At night, ensure the fires are large and bright. Always have enough fuel on hand to keep the fires burning consistently and be prepared to maintain them for as long as necessary.

Mirrors and reflective surfaces are another effective signaling tool. A signal mirror can reflect sunlight over long distances, catching the eye of a potential rescuer. Practice aiming the mirror by using the sun's reflection to create a flash of light. Hold the mirror at an angle to the sun and aim the reflected light toward your target by looking through the sighting hole. This technique can be surprisingly effective, and a well-aimed flash can be seen from miles away.

In addition to mirrors, other shiny objects, such as the reflective lining of a space blanket or even the face of a wristwatch, can serve a similar purpose. Always carry a signal mirror in your survival kit, as its lightweight and compact nature makes it an invaluable tool for attracting attention. Whistles are a straightforward and reliable signaling method. Unlike shouting, which can quickly tire you out and may not carry far, a whistle's high-pitched sound can travel long distances. Use a whistle to create a pattern of three short blasts, which is an internationally recognized distress signal. Repeat this pattern at regular intervals to increase the chances of being heard. A whistle is also effective in situations where visibility is poor, such as in dense forests or during heavy snowfall.

If you have access to a flashlight or other light source, signaling at night becomes more manageable. Use the light to create an SOS signal: three short flashes, followed by three long flashes, and then three short flashes again. This Morse code for SOS is widely understood and can be seen from a considerable distance. Similarly, if you have a laser pointer, it can serve as a signaling device in low-light conditions.

Sometimes, the environment itself can be used to your advantage for signaling. Large ground-to-air signals can be constructed using natural materials. Create large symbols like an "X" or "SOS" on the ground using rocks, logs, or other contrasting materials. These symbols should be at least three meters in length to be visible from the air. Clear an area of snow, sand, or vegetation to create a stark contrast that can be seen by passing aircraft or search parties.

In snowy conditions, stomp out large letters or symbols in the snow, and in sandy or grassy areas, use branches or rocks to form your signal. The key is to ensure the signal stands out against the natural background. Regularly check and maintain these ground signals to ensure they remain visible and intact.

Color can also play a crucial role in signaling. Bright colors that contrast with the natural surroundings, such as orange or red, are ideal for attracting attention. Carrying a brightly colored piece of fabric or plastic sheeting in your survival kit can serve multiple purposes, including signaling for help. Spread the fabric on the ground or hang it from a tree to make your presence known.

Modern technology offers additional signaling options that can significantly enhance your chances of being rescued. Personal locator beacons (PLBs) and satellite messengers are invaluable tools in the wilderness.

A PLB is a compact device that, when activated, sends a distress signal with your GPS coordinates to emergency services via satellite. This can drastically reduce the time it takes for rescuers to locate you. Similarly, satellite messengers can send pre-set or custom messages to predetermined contacts, providing updates on your location and status. These devices are a lifeline in remote areas where traditional communication methods are unavailable.

Cell phones, while not always reliable in remote areas, should not be overlooked. If you have a signal, a phone can be used to call for help or send text messages, which sometimes go through even when voice calls do not. Even if you're out of range, periodically checking for a signal when on higher ground or in open areas can sometimes provide the opportunity to call for help.

Another method involves using sound. Beyond whistles, improvised noise-makers can be created from materials at hand. Banging rocks together, using a stick to strike a hollow log, or creating a makeshift drum can produce loud sounds that might attract attention. Regular, rhythmic sounds are more likely to be noticed than random noise. It's also crucial to stay aware of your environment and any potential rescue operations. If you hear aircraft or see search parties, use whatever signaling method you have at your disposal to draw attention to your location. Waving a brightly colored item, flashing a mirror, or creating loud noises can make a significant difference. Stay vigilant and ready to signal at a moment's notice.

Understanding the behavior of search and rescue teams can also aid in your signaling strategy. Rescuers are trained to look for signs of human presence, so anything out of the ordinary can catch their attention. A line of rocks in a straight formation, a signal fire, or bright colors contrasting with the natural environment can all serve as indicators. Familiarize yourself with common rescue protocols and practices, so you know what to expect and how best to assist in your own rescue.

In a group setting, coordinating signaling efforts is essential. Assign roles to different members to manage fires, mirrors, and other signaling devices, ensuring that efforts are sustained and organized. Communication within the group about the status of signaling efforts and any sightings of potential rescuers will keep everyone aligned and efficient. Maintaining a positive mindset and not giving in to despair is critical. Effective signaling requires persistence and patience. It might take time for rescuers to spot you, especially in challenging environments, so continuous effort is necessary. Rotate duties among group members to avoid burnout and ensure that signals are maintained without interruption.

3. SURVIVAL KIT ESSENTIALS

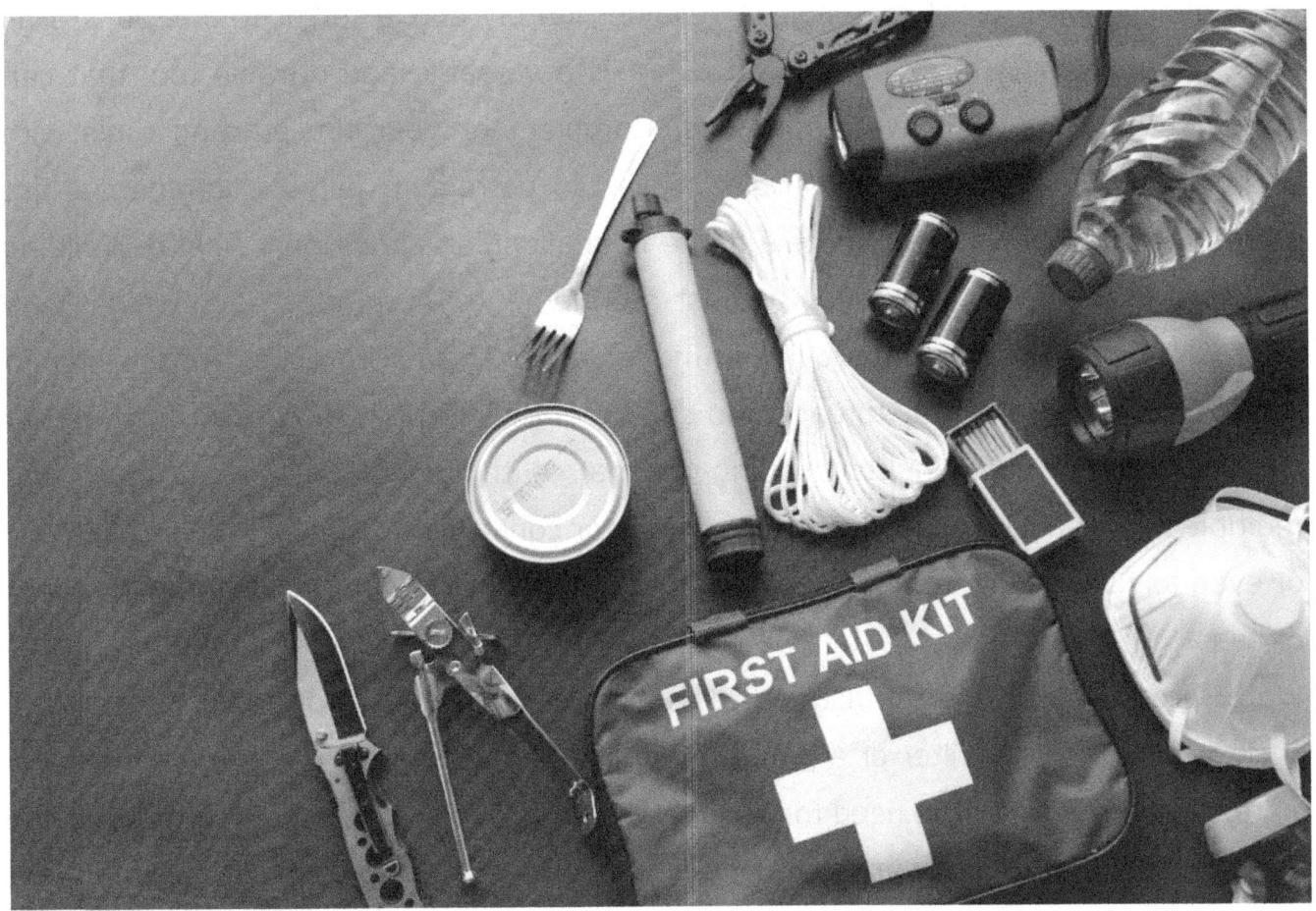

3.1 CHOOSING YOUR TOOLS

In the wild, your survival kit is your lifeline, a collection of tools that can make the difference between life and death. Choosing the right tools for your kit is a strategic decision that requires careful consideration of your environment, potential challenges, and personal skills. Every item should serve a purpose, adding value to your ability to survive and thrive in unpredictable conditions.

The cornerstone of any survival kit is a good knife. A knife is not just a tool; it's an extension of your hand, enabling you to perform a multitude of tasks, from building shelter and preparing food to crafting other tools. When choosing a knife, consider its durability, versatility, and ease of maintenance. A full-tang, fixed-blade knife is generally more robust than a folding knife, providing greater strength and reliability. Look for a blade made of high-quality stainless steel or carbon steel, which can withstand heavy use and hold a sharp edge. The handle should offer a comfortable grip, reducing the risk of injury during prolonged use. Fire-making tools are another critical component. Fire provides warmth, cooks food, purifies water, and serves as a signaling device. Multiple fire-starting methods should be included to ensure redundancy. Waterproof matches, a reliable lighter, and a ferrocerium rod are all excellent choices. A ferro rod, in particular, is a versatile and durable tool that can produce sparks even in wet conditions. Complement your fire-starting tools with tinder materials, such as cotton balls soaked in petroleum jelly or commercial fire starters, to ensure you can ignite a flame in challenging conditions. Shelter-building tools are essential for protection against the elements. A compact, lightweight tarp or emergency bivvy bag can provide immediate shelter and protection from wind and rain. These items are easy to pack and can be quickly deployed. Paracord is another versatile tool in your shelter-building arsenal. With its high tensile strength and multiple inner strands, paracord can be used for constructing shelters, securing gear, or even as fishing line. Carry at least 50 feet of paracord in your kit to cover a variety of uses.

Water procurement and purification tools are indispensable. A portable water filter, such as a straw-style filter or a pump filter, allows you to drink directly from natural water sources without the need for boiling. Water purification tablets or drops provide a lightweight backup, ensuring you have safe drinking water even if your primary filter fails. Include a metal container for boiling water; it can also be used for cooking and as a makeshift signal mirror.

Navigation tools help you find your way and avoid getting lost. A quality compass and a topographic map of your area are fundamental. Learn to use these tools effectively before heading into the wild. A GPS device or a smartphone with offline maps can provide additional navigation assistance, but always rely primarily on non-electronic tools, as batteries can fail. A signal mirror and a whistle should also be part of your navigation and signaling toolkit, enabling you to attract attention if needed. First aid supplies are crucial for addressing injuries and illnesses in the field. A well-stocked first aid kit should include bandages, antiseptic wipes, adhesive tape, tweezers, and pain relievers. Consider including items specific to your environment, such as snake bite kits or blister treatments. Knowledge of basic first aid procedures is equally important, so take the time to learn how to use each item in your kit effectively. Lighting tools extend your capability to function in low-light conditions. A reliable headlamp or flashlight with extra batteries ensures you can navigate and perform tasks after dark. Opt for LED lights, which are more energy-efficient and durable. Include spare batteries and consider a small, solar-powered charger to keep electronic devices operational.

Food procurement tools can supplement your supplies and provide sustenance if you're in the wilderness for an extended period. A small fishing kit, including hooks, lines, and sinkers, can help you catch fish. A wire saw or compact folding saw aids in building traps and processing wood for fires. Knowledge of local edible plants and how to harvest them safely is invaluable, turning the natural environment into a food source. Repair and maintenance tools keep your gear functional and in good condition. A multitool with pliers, screwdrivers, and cutting implements can address various repair needs. Duct tape and sewing kits are also useful for fixing torn clothing, broken gear, or making temporary repairs to your shelter.

Personal items tailored to your specific needs round out your survival kit. These might include prescription medications, personal hygiene items, or a survival guidebook specific to your region. Every survival situation is unique, and personalizing your kit ensures you are prepared for the challenges you are most likely to face.

The process of choosing your tools is not just about selecting items; it's about understanding how each tool integrates into your overall survival strategy. Practice using each item in controlled conditions to become familiar with its functionality and limitations. Regularly review and update your kit, replacing expired items and adapting to any new survival knowledge or changes in your environment.

3.2 MULTI-USE ITEMS YOU MUST HAVE

In the wilderness, every item in your survival kit should serve multiple functions, maximizing your efficiency and adaptability. Multi-use items are invaluable, providing versatile solutions to a variety of challenges you may face. Selecting these items with care ensures that your kit remains compact and lightweight while still equipping you to handle diverse situations. One of the most essential multi-use items is a good-quality bandana. This simple piece of cloth has an astonishing array of uses. It can serve as a makeshift bandage or sling in case of injury, a head covering to protect against the sun, or a filter to strain sediment from water. When soaked in water, it can help keep you cool, and when dry, it can be used as a fire starter. The bandana can also be used to tie things together, mark trails, or signal for help with its bright color. Its versatility makes it a small but powerful addition to your survival kit. Duct tape is another indispensable multi-use item. Known for its incredible strength and adhesion, duct tape can be used to repair almost anything. From fixing broken gear and sealing holes in your shelter to creating splints and securing bandages, its applications are nearly endless. You can use duct tape to waterproof items, make a rope, or even fashion a quick pair of makeshift shoes if necessary. Despite its bulk, carrying a small roll or wrapping some around a water bottle or lighter ensures you always have this valuable resource at hand.

A stainless steel water bottle is not only for hydration but also serves multiple survival functions. It can be used to boil water for purification, cook food, or even as a container to carry items. The durability of stainless steel means it can withstand the rigors of the wild, and its capacity to hold both hot and cold liquids adds to its utility. In a pinch, it can be used as a signaling device by reflecting sunlight or making noise. A water bottle is more than just a vessel; it's a multipurpose tool essential for survival.

Paracord, or parachute cord, is another item that offers extraordinary versatility. With a high tensile strength and multiple inner strands, paracord can be used for building shelters, making snares and traps, creating a bow drill for fire starting, or even fashioning fishing lines. The inner strands can be used for sewing repairs, flossing, or as tinder for starting fires. Whether you need to secure gear, construct a stretcher, or set up a tarp, paracord's adaptability makes it a must-have in your kit.

Aluminum foil is lightweight and compact but incredibly versatile. It can be used to cook food directly over a fire, as a makeshift container for boiling water, or to reflect heat. Aluminum foil can also be fashioned into a signal mirror, used to protect food from animals, or even employed in creating a solar oven. Its flexibility and range of uses make it an excellent addition to any survival kit.

A multi-tool is the epitome of a multi-use item. Featuring various tools such as pliers, knives, screwdrivers, and scissors, a high-quality multi-tool can address a myriad of needs. It's perfect for gear repair, food preparation, first aid, and numerous other tasks. The compact design ensures that you have a toolbox worth of functionality in a single, portable item. Whether you need to cut wood, open a can, or repair your equipment, a multi-tool is an essential component of any survival kit.

Plastic bags, particularly heavy-duty ones like ziplock or contractor bags, are incredibly useful. They can be used to collect and carry water, protect gear from moisture, or serve as makeshift gloves. Large bags can be used as emergency ponchos, ground covers, or even as part of a makeshift shelter. In addition, plastic bags can help with foraging, creating solar stills, or storing food and other supplies. Their versatility and light weight make them an excellent choice for any survival scenario.

A tarp is another indispensable multi-use item that can serve as a shelter, ground cover, or rain catchment system. It can protect you from the elements, be used to collect water, or act as a signal due to its large surface area. When constructing a shelter, a tarp provides a quick and effective solution, offering insulation and protection. Its durability and multiple applications make it a valuable addition to your kit. Safety pins, though small, offer significant versatility. They can be used to repair clothing, secure bandages, create fishing hooks, or attach gear. In a pinch, safety pins can be used as part of a snare trap or to create a makeshift zipper pull. Their small size and light weight make it easy to carry several, ensuring you have them available for various unexpected uses. Lastly, a simple mirror, besides its obvious use for signaling, can help start a fire by focusing sunlight. It can also be used for personal grooming, which is crucial for morale and hygiene in survival situations. A mirror can assist in medical situations, allowing you to inspect wounds in hard-to-see places.

3.3 PACKING FOR WEIGHT AND EFFICIENCY

Packing for weight and efficiency is a critical aspect of wilderness survival. The balance between carrying enough gear to ensure your safety and comfort and keeping your pack light enough to move swiftly and efficiently can be challenging. The goal is to create a survival kit that is compact, lightweight, and comprehensive, ensuring you are prepared for any situation without being bogged down by unnecessary items. The foundation of efficient packing starts with selecting a high-quality backpack designed for your needs. Look for a pack that is durable, water-resistant, and comfortable, with adjustable straps and ample padding. A well-fitted pack distributes weight evenly across your body, reducing strain and fatigue. Compartments and external straps are also useful for organizing your gear and keeping frequently used items easily accessible. Begin by prioritizing the essential items that will address your core survival needs: shelter, water, fire, and food. Each item you pack should serve multiple functions whenever possible to minimize weight while maximizing utility. For example, a multi-tool can replace several single-use tools, and a lightweight tarp can provide shelter, ground cover, and a means to collect rainwater.

When packing, consider the weight and bulk of each item. Choose lightweight alternatives to heavy equipment where possible. For instance, opt for a compact, collapsible stove instead of a bulky one, or a titanium spork instead of traditional cutlery. Every ounce saved adds up over time, making a significant difference in your pack's overall weight.

Organization within your pack is crucial for efficiency. Use smaller pouches or packing cubes to group related items together. This method not only keeps your gear organized but also allows for quick access to necessary items without unpacking everything. For example, keep all your fire-starting tools in one pouch and first aid supplies in another. This compartmentalization makes it easier to find what you need, especially in emergencies.

Your shelter system should be lightweight yet effective. A compact tent, a bivvy sack, or a simple tarp can provide sufficient protection from the elements without adding unnecessary bulk. Consider the climate and terrain you will encounter and choose a shelter that meets those specific needs. Remember, an efficient shelter setup not only saves weight but also time and energy when setting up camp.

Water is a non-negotiable necessity, and your method of carrying and purifying water should reflect this. Collapsible water bottles or hydration bladders are excellent choices because they take up minimal space when empty. Pair these with a reliable water purification system, such as a small filter or purification tablets. A lightweight metal container for boiling water can serve multiple purposes, including cooking and signal reflection.

Fire-starting tools are essential for warmth, cooking, and signaling. Pack a variety of fire-starting methods, such as waterproof matches, a lighter, and a ferrocerium rod, to ensure redundancy. Include lightweight tinder, like cotton balls soaked in petroleum jelly, stored in a small waterproof container. These items are light but invaluable, providing you with multiple ways to start a fire in different conditions.

Food and nutrition are critical, especially during extended periods in the wild. Opt for lightweight, high-calorie foods that provide sustained energy. Freeze-dried meals, protein bars, and nuts are excellent choices. Pack these in resealable bags to save space and reduce waste. Additionally, carrying a small fishing kit or snare wire can provide supplementary food sources with minimal weight.

Clothing should be chosen based on the principle of layering, allowing you to adjust to varying weather conditions. Lightweight, moisture-wicking base layers, insulating mid-layers, and a waterproof outer layer provide flexibility without excessive weight. Pack spare socks and underwear in waterproof bags to keep them dry. Remember, clothing also includes items like hats and gloves, which are small but essential for maintaining body heat.

Medical supplies are another critical component. A compact first aid kit should include bandages, antiseptics, pain relievers, and any personal medications. Consider the specific risks of your environment and pack accordingly—snake bite kits for areas with venomous snakes or insect repellent for bug-prone regions. A small, lightweight emergency manual can also be invaluable for providing guidance on medical emergencies and survival techniques. Navigation tools, such as a map, compass, and GPS device, are essential for ensuring you can find your way. Keep these items in a waterproof bag and make sure they are easily accessible. Knowledge of how to use these tools is as important as carrying them, so take time to familiarize yourself with their functions before heading out.

For additional survival gear, consider the weight-to-utility ratio carefully. Items like a compact solar charger can keep your electronic devices operational without the need for heavy batteries. A lightweight sewing kit can repair torn clothing and gear, extending their usability. Safety pins, duct tape, and a small roll of strong cordage can be used for numerous repairs and improvisations.

Finally, test your pack before setting out. Load it with your gear and take it on a trial hike to ensure it feels balanced and manageable. Adjust the contents as necessary, removing items that are not essential and replacing heavier items with lighter alternatives. This practice run can help you identify any potential issues and refine your packing strategy.

BOOK 2: MASTERY OF FIRE AND COOKING

1. FIRE BUILDING TECHNIQUES

1.1 TRADITIONAL AND MODERN FIRE STARTING METHODS

Fire is an indispensable element in wilderness survival, providing warmth, cooking capabilities, and a means to purify water. The ability to start a fire using both traditional and modern methods is a critical skill for any survivalist. Understanding the nuances of these techniques ensures you are prepared for any situation, regardless of the tools at your disposal.

Traditional Fire Starting Methods

Traditional fire starting methods are rooted in history, used by our ancestors long before the advent of modern conveniences. Mastering these techniques not only connects us to the past but also guarantees you can start a fire even when modern tools fail.

Friction-Based Methods

1. **Hand Drill** The hand drill is one of the most primitive fire-starting methods.

It requires a spindle (a straight, dry stick) and a fireboard (a flat piece of wood with a notch and a depression). By placing the spindle in the depression and rolling it between your hands with downward pressure, you create friction. This friction generates heat, eventually producing a small ember. The ember is then transferred to a tinder bundle, where gentle blowing ignites the tinder.

2. **Bow Drill** The bow drill is a more advanced friction method that uses a bow to rotate the spindle, making it easier to maintain speed and pressure. The bow is a curved piece of wood strung with cordage. The spindle is placed in a socket on the fireboard, and the bowstring is wrapped around it. Moving the bow back and forth spins the spindle rapidly, creating an ember in the notch of the fireboard. This ember is then carefully placed in a tinder bundle and blown into flame.

Percussion-Based Methods

1. **Flint and Steel** Striking flint against steel produces sparks that can ignite a tinder bundle. The flint is typically a hard, sharp-edged rock, while the steel is a specially hardened piece of metal. This method requires practice to achieve the correct angle and force to produce consistent sparks. Historically, char cloth (a piece of fabric that has been partially burned to create a highly combustible material) was used as tinder, but any dry, fibrous material will work.

2. **Fire Plough** The fire plough involves rubbing a hardwood stick (the plough) along a groove in a softer wood fireboard. The friction creates small particles of wood that ignite from the heat generated. This method is less efficient than the bow drill or hand drill but can be effective with practice.

Modern Fire Starting Methods

Modern fire starting methods leverage advanced materials and technology to make fire starting more reliable and accessible. These tools are designed to be easy to use and effective in various conditions, providing an essential backup to traditional methods.

Chemical and Spark-Based Methods

1. **Lighters** Butane lighters are the most convenient fire-starting tools available. They produce a steady flame with minimal effort. Windproof lighters, such as those made by Zippo, are particularly useful in harsh weather conditions. Always carry a backup lighter and keep it dry to ensure it functions when needed.

2. **Matches** Waterproof matches and stormproof matches are designed to ignite even in wet or windy conditions. Store matches in a waterproof container to protect them from moisture. Strike-anywhere matches can be ignited on a variety of surfaces, offering versatility in the field.

3. **Ferrocerium Rods** Also known as ferro rods or firesteel, these rods produce sparks when scraped with a metal striker. The sparks reach temperatures of around 3,000 degrees Fahrenheit, hot enough to ignite most tinder materials. Ferro rods are reliable in wet conditions and are a favorite among survivalists for their durability and effectiveness.

4. **Magnesium Fire Starters** These tools combine a block of magnesium with a ferro rod. Shavings from the magnesium block are highly flammable and can be ignited with sparks from the ferro rod. Magnesium fire starters are particularly useful for creating a fire in damp conditions, as the shavings burn at a very high temperature.

Electric-Based Methods

1. **Electric Arc Lighters** These lighters use a small electric arc to ignite materials. They are rechargeable via USB and function well in windy conditions. However, they depend on battery power, so it's crucial to monitor their charge and carry a backup power source, such as a solar charger.

Selecting the Right Method

Choosing the right fire-starting method depends on your environment, available materials, and personal proficiency. It's wise to carry multiple fire-starting tools to ensure redundancy. Practice each method to build confidence and efficiency. Here are a few considerations:

- **Environment**: In wet or windy conditions, waterproof matches, lighters, and ferro rods are more reliable than friction-based methods.

- **Materials**: Ensure you have access to suitable tinder. Natural materials like dry grass, bark, and leaves work well. Prepared tinder, such as cotton balls soaked in petroleum jelly, provides a consistent and effective option.

- **Skill Level**: Traditional methods require more skill and patience. Regular practice improves success rates. Modern methods are generally easier and faster, making them ideal for emergency situations.

Building and Maintaining the Fire

Once you have a flame, the next step is to build and maintain your fire. Start with small, dry tinder and gradually add kindling—thin sticks that catch fire easily. Once the kindling is burning well, add larger pieces of wood. Arrange the wood in a teepee, lean-to, or log cabin structure to allow airflow, which helps the fire burn hotter and more efficiently.

Keep your fire small and manageable. Large fires consume more resources and are harder to control. Always have water or dirt nearby to extinguish the fire if it spreads. Never leave a fire unattended and ensure it is completely out before leaving the area.

1.2 MAINTAINING A FIRE IN ADVERSE CONDITIONS

Maintaining a fire in adverse conditions is one of the most challenging yet vital skills in wilderness survival. Whether you're dealing with wind, rain, snow, or limited resources, keeping a fire alive can mean the difference between warmth and cold, cooked food and raw, safety and exposure. Understanding how to adapt to and overcome these obstacles is essential.

Wind

Wind can be both a friend and a foe when it comes to fire. While a gentle breeze can help fan the flames and provide necessary oxygen, strong winds can quickly extinguish a fire or scatter embers, posing a risk of wildfires. To manage wind, the first step is to choose a sheltered location. Look for natural windbreaks like large rocks, fallen logs, or dense vegetation that can protect your fire from direct gusts. Building a windbreak around your fire is another effective strategy. Use logs, stones, or even a tarp to create a barrier. This not only protects the fire but also helps concentrate heat. Arrange your windbreak in a U-shape, with the open end facing away from the wind. This configuration allows air to flow into the fire while shielding it from the strongest gusts.

When setting up the fire itself, consider digging a shallow pit. This not only shields the fire from the wind but also helps retain heat. Place large rocks around the pit's perimeter to further stabilize and protect the flames. These rocks will also absorb heat, which can be radiated back into your shelter, providing additional warmth.

Rain

Rain presents a unique challenge, as it can easily extinguish a fire and soak your tinder and kindling. To combat rain, start by creating a dry work area. Use a tarp, poncho, or large leaves to cover your fire pit and keep your materials dry. If possible, build your fire under a natural canopy or a makeshift shelter.

Selecting the right tinder and kindling is crucial in wet conditions. Look for materials that are naturally resistant to moisture, such as birch bark, which contains oils that help it burn even when damp. Alternatively, carry a supply of waterproof tinder, such as commercial fire starters or homemade options like cotton balls soaked in petroleum jelly.

Building a base of dry materials can also help. Place a layer of dry sticks, bark, or even a piece of dry wood on the ground before constructing your fire. This base layer will keep your tinder and kindling off the wet ground and help ignite the fire more easily. Once the fire is lit, maintaining it in the rain requires constant attention. Use larger logs to create a teepee or log cabin structure that will shield the core of the fire from raindrops. Keep adding dry fuel to the center of the fire, ensuring that the outer layers protect the inner flame. Additionally, a large, reflective barrier can be set up on the side opposite the wind to protect the fire from the rain and reflect heat back towards it.

Snow and Cold

Snow and cold present their own set of challenges. The first task is to clear away any snow from your fire site, digging down to the bare ground if possible. If this isn't feasible, create a platform using logs or rocks to elevate your fire above the snow. This prevents the fire from sinking into the snow and being extinguished by melting water. Building a reflector wall behind the fire can significantly enhance its effectiveness in cold conditions. This wall, constructed from logs or stones, reflects heat back towards you, making your shelter area warmer. Additionally, use a teepee or log cabin fire structure to create a concentrated core of heat that is easier to maintain.

In extreme cold, keeping a fire burning consistently is vital. Gather plenty of firewood before nightfall, as searching for fuel in the dark can be difficult and dangerous. Use larger logs that will burn longer and provide sustained heat. If you have access to green wood, use it sparingly on the outer edges of the fire to prolong the burn time while keeping the core fire fueled with dry wood.

Limited Resources

When resources are scarce, efficiency and ingenuity become paramount. Prioritize finding the most effective tinder and kindling available. Dry, dead wood from standing trees is preferable to wood found on the ground, as it is less likely to be damp.

Maximize the efficiency of your fire by constructing it with care. A small, well-built fire can be more effective than a large, poorly managed one. Use the "star fire" method, where the ends of large logs are pushed into the center of the fire as they burn, conserving fuel and maintaining a steady heat source.

In situations where fuel is extremely limited, consider using a Dakota fire hole. This technique involves digging two connected holes in the ground: one for the fire and one for air intake. The design draws air into the fire pit, creating an efficient burn that requires less fuel and produces less smoke, making it ideal for conserving resources.

Practical Tips for All Conditions

- **Preparation**: Always have a supply of dry tinder stored in a waterproof container. This could include items like dryer lint, cotton balls soaked in petroleum jelly, or commercial fire starters. This preparation ensures you have reliable materials to start a fire quickly.

- **Layering**: Build your fire in layers, starting with small, dry tinder, then adding progressively larger kindling and fuel. This method ensures that the fire builds steadily and remains strong.

- **Maintenance**: Once your fire is established, feed it regularly with dry wood. Avoid adding too much fuel at once, as this can smother the fire. Instead, add wood gradually to maintain a steady burn.

- **Wind and Rain Protection**: Always be mindful of changing weather conditions. Adjust your windbreaks and shelters as needed to protect your fire from the elements. In particularly harsh weather, consider building multiple smaller fires to ensure at least one remains burning.

1.3 FIRE SAFETY IN THE WILDERNESS

Fire is a fundamental tool for survival in the wilderness, providing warmth, a means to cook food, purify water, and a source of light. However, with its many benefits comes a significant responsibility: fire safety. Ensuring that your fire remains under control and does not become a hazard is critical. Understanding and implementing fire safety practices is essential for protecting yourself, others, and the environment. The first step in fire safety begins with selecting an appropriate site for your fire. Choose a location that is at least 15 feet away from tents, trees, shrubs, and any flammable materials. Clear the area of any dry grass, leaves, and other debris that could catch fire. If possible, use an existing fire ring or pit to minimize the impact on the environment and reduce the risk of an uncontrolled fire. If you need to create a new fire pit, dig a small hole or build a ring of rocks to contain the fire.

Before lighting your fire, always check the local regulations and fire danger levels. Many areas have restrictions during dry seasons or periods of high fire risk. Abiding by these regulations not only keeps you safe but also helps prevent wildfires. If fire bans are in place, consider alternative methods for cooking and staying warm, such as using a portable stove. Once you have prepared your fire site, gather your materials. Use dry, seasoned wood to minimize smoke and ensure a clean burn. Green or wet wood can produce excessive smoke and is more difficult to ignite, leading to frustration and wasted resources. Start with small tinder and kindling, gradually adding larger pieces of wood as the fire establishes. This method ensures that your fire builds steadily and remains manageable.

Maintaining control over your fire is crucial. Keep the fire small and contained within the fire ring or pit. A smaller fire is easier to manage and less likely to spread. Never leave your fire unattended, even for a short period. Assign someone to monitor the fire at all times, especially if you are in a group. This watchful eye can quickly address any issues that arise, such as stray embers or changes in wind direction.

Wind is a significant factor in fire safety. Gusts can carry embers far from the fire, igniting nearby vegetation or debris. To mitigate this risk, build a windbreak using rocks or logs around the fire. This barrier helps contain embers and maintains the fire's intensity. Additionally, always be aware of changing weather conditions and be prepared to extinguish the fire quickly if the wind picks up.

Water and soil are your best allies in controlling and extinguishing a fire. Always have a bucket of water, sand, or dirt nearby to douse the fire if it begins to spread or when you are ready to extinguish it. To put out a fire, start by sprinkling water over the flames, then stir the ashes with a stick to expose hot spots. Continue adding water and stirring until the fire is completely out. Use the back of your hand to feel for heat over the ashes—if it's still warm, it needs more water or dirt.

In the unfortunate event of a burn, knowing basic first aid is essential. Cool the burn immediately with running water or a wet cloth to reduce pain and swelling. Do not use ice, as it can cause further tissue damage. Cover the burn with a clean, non-stick bandage and seek medical attention if necessary. Having a well-stocked first aid kit and knowing how to use it can make a significant difference in managing injuries. One often overlooked aspect of fire safety is the impact on the environment. Fires can cause long-term damage to vegetation and soil. Practicing Leave No Trace principles helps minimize your impact. Use established fire rings when available, burn wood down to ash, and scatter cool ashes over a wide area. If you must create a new fire site, restore the area to its natural state before leaving. Preventing the spread of wildfires is not only about managing your campfire but also about understanding and mitigating risks. Avoid building fires during dry, windy conditions, and always have a plan for emergency situations. Create a buffer zone around your fire by clearing vegetation and using rocks or dirt to contain it. Be mindful of the materials you burn; never use accelerants like gasoline, which can cause explosive flames and are difficult to control. The tools you use can also contribute to fire safety. A shovel, bucket, and fire-resistant gloves are essential items for managing and extinguishing your fire. A shovel can help you dig a fire pit, create a windbreak, and bury hot ashes. Fire-resistant gloves protect your hands when handling hot objects or adding wood to the fire. Education is a powerful tool in fire safety. Teach everyone in your group, especially children, about the importance of fire safety and the proper techniques for building and maintaining a fire. Demonstrating safe practices not only ensures their safety but also instills a respect for the environment and the power of fire.

2. Cooking in the Wild

2.1 Preparing Game and Fish

Before setting out to hunt or fish, it's crucial to understand the ecosystem around you. Different environments offer various types of game and fish, each requiring specific techniques for preparation. Familiarize yourself with local wildlife regulations to ensure you hunt and fish legally and sustainably. Knowing the habits and habitats of your potential prey increases your chances of a successful catch.

Field Dressing Game

Once you've successfully hunted game, the next step is field dressing. This process begins as soon as the animal is downed to prevent spoilage and make the carcass easier to transport. The key to efficient field dressing is having the right tools and a steady hand.

Step-by-Step Process:

1. **Bleeding the Animal**: Start by bleeding the animal to ensure the meat is clean and palatable. This involves cutting the major blood vessels in the neck or heart area. Allow the blood to drain completely.

2. **Opening the Carcass**: Lay the animal on its back and make a careful incision from the chest to the pelvis. Avoid puncturing the stomach or intestines to prevent contamination. Use a sharp knife and cut through the skin and membrane.

3. **Removing the Organs**: Gently remove the internal organs, starting with the digestive system. Work carefully around the heart and lungs, keeping them intact if you plan to use them. Check the liver for any signs of disease, which could indicate the meat is unsafe to eat.

4. **Cooling the Meat**: In warm conditions, it's essential to cool the meat quickly to prevent spoilage. Hang the carcass in a shaded, airy location or place it on a bed of leaves to allow air circulation.

Field dressing requires practice and precision. Over time, you'll develop a technique that works best for you, ensuring the meat remains uncontaminated and fresh.

Butchering Game

After field dressing, the next step is butchering the animal into manageable pieces. This process varies depending on the size and type of game, but the principles remain the same.

1. **Quartering the Carcass**: Start by quartering the animal into more manageable pieces: front legs, hind legs, and torso. This makes it easier to handle and cook.

2. **Removing the Hide**: Skinning the animal can be done either before or after quartering, depending on the size of the game. Larger animals are often easier to skin after quartering. Make incisions around the joints and peel back the hide, using your knife to separate it from the flesh.

3. **Deboning and Trimming**: Remove the major bones and trim any excess fat. While some fat is desirable for cooking, too much can make the meat greasy. Use a sharp knife to cut along the bone, preserving as much meat as possible.

4. **Portioning the Meat**: Cut the meat into portions suitable for cooking. Consider how you plan to cook each piece – larger cuts are ideal for roasting over a fire, while smaller pieces can be used for stews or grilling.

Preparing Fish

Fishing is often a more reliable source of food than hunting, especially near water bodies. Once you've caught fish, the preparation process ensures the meat is clean and safe to eat.

1. **Cleaning the Fish**: Begin by scaling the fish. Hold the fish firmly and use the back of your knife to scrape from tail to head, removing all scales. Rinse the fish in clean water.

2. **Gutting the Fish**: Make an incision along the belly from the anus to the gills. Remove the internal organs, being careful not to puncture the intestines. Rinse the cavity thoroughly to remove any blood or debris.

3. **Filleting the Fish**: Lay the fish on its side and make a cut behind the gills, down to the backbone. Turn the knife and slice along the backbone, removing the fillet. Repeat on the other side. Smaller fish can be cooked whole, while larger fish are easier to handle as fillets.

4. **Removing Bones**: For boneless fillets, use tweezers to pull out any remaining pin bones. This step ensures a pleasant eating experience and reduces the risk of choking on small bones.

Cooking Techniques

Cooking game and fish over an open fire requires some skill but can yield delicious results. The key is to control the heat and cook the meat evenly.

1. **Roasting**: Roasting on a spit is ideal for larger cuts of game. Secure the meat on a sturdy stick or spit, and rotate it slowly over the fire. This method allows the meat to cook evenly, retaining its juices and flavor.

2. **Grilling**: For smaller cuts or fish fillets, grilling on a flat rock or grill grate over the fire works well. Ensure the surface is hot before placing the meat, and cook it quickly to prevent drying out.

3. **Stewing**: Using a pot or makeshift container, stew meat and fish with foraged herbs and vegetables. This method is excellent for tough cuts of meat, as the slow cooking process tenderizes the meat and infuses it with flavor.

4. **Smoking**: Smoking meat and fish not only cooks them but also preserves them for future use. Create a smoking rack above a low, smoldering fire and let the smoke cure the meat slowly. This process can take several hours but results in

highly flavorful, preserved food.

2.2 PLANT-BASED COOKING OPTIONS

Cooking in the wild often brings to mind images of roasting meat over an open fire, but plant-based cooking options are equally crucial for a balanced diet and can often be easier to procure. Understanding which plants are edible, how to harvest them, and the best ways to prepare them is essential for survival and adds variety to your wilderness meals.

Foraging for Edible Plants

Foraging is a skill that requires knowledge and practice. The wilderness is filled with edible plants, but also with toxic ones. Proper identification is paramount. Always cross-reference your finds with a reliable field guide, and when in doubt, do not consume the plant. Common edible plants include dandelions, wild garlic, and various berries, each offering unique flavors and nutritional benefits. Dandelions, for instance, are ubiquitous and entirely edible. The leaves can be eaten raw or cooked, the flowers can be battered and fried, and the roots can be roasted to make a coffee substitute. Wild garlic is another excellent find, with both its leaves and bulbs providing a potent, savory flavor that enhances any dish. Berries such as blackberries, raspberries, and blueberries are not only delicious but packed with vitamins. These can be eaten fresh, dried for later use, or cooked into a wild berry compote. Always ensure berries are properly identified, as some, like nightshade berries, are highly toxic.

Harvesting and Preparing Wild Plants

Harvesting wild plants requires care and respect for the environment. Only take what you need, and always leave enough behind for the plant to continue thriving. Use a sharp knife or scissors to cut plants cleanly, avoiding damage that could lead to disease or death.

Once harvested, plants should be thoroughly cleaned. Rinse leaves and roots in clean water to remove dirt and insects. Some plants, like nettles, require special handling to remove stings—boiling or blanching neutralizes the irritants.

Cooking Techniques for Wild Plants

Cooking wild plants enhances their flavors and makes some more palatable and digestible. Here are some techniques to consider:

Boiling

Boiling is a straightforward method suitable for many wild greens. It softens tough leaves and stems, making them easier to eat. For example, dandelion greens can be boiled to reduce their bitterness. Simply bring a pot of water to a boil, add the greens, and cook until tender.

Steaming

Steaming preserves more nutrients than boiling and enhances the natural flavors of the plants. A simple setup involves placing a small amount of water in the bottom of a pot, adding a steaming rack or improvising with stones and sticks, and covering with a lid or large leaves. Steam greens, roots, and even flower buds for a nutritious meal.

Roasting

Roasting brings out the natural sugars in roots and tubers, providing a hearty, flavorful dish. Wrap roots like dandelion or burdock in foil and place them in the embers of your fire. Roast until tender, then peel and enjoy. This method is also excellent for nuts, which can be roasted to enhance their flavor and make them easier to shell.

Sautéing

Sautéing in a bit of oil or fat (if available) can add richness to wild plants. Use a flat rock or a portable pan over the fire. Add chopped greens, garlic, and any other foraged herbs to the pan and cook until wilted and fragrant. This technique works well with wild garlic, ramps, and young nettle leaves.

Drying

Drying is an excellent method for preserving plants. Hang herbs like mint, thyme, and sage in a dry, airy location or use a low-heat method near your fire. Dried herbs can be used to season other dishes or brewed into teas. Berries can be sun-dried or dried near a gentle heat source, providing a nutritious snack or ingredient for later.

Combining Plants with Other Foraged Foods

Pairing plants with other foraged foods can create more balanced and flavorful meals. Wild grains, mushrooms, and even insects can complement your plant-based dishes. For example, mushrooms sautéed with wild garlic and dandelion greens create a hearty, nutritious meal. Ensure mushrooms are correctly identified, as many are toxic.

Insects, though not commonly consumed in many cultures, are a rich protein source. Grasshoppers and crickets can be roasted and added to plant dishes for added nutrition. They may require some psychological adjustment, but in survival situations, they can be a valuable food source. Wild plants are not only a source of calories but also provide essential vitamins and minerals. Greens like nettles and dandelion are rich in iron, calcium, and vitamins A and C. Berries provide antioxidants and fiber, while nuts and seeds offer healthy fats and protein. Balancing your diet with a variety of foraged plants ensures you receive a broad spectrum of nutrients. It's essential to vary your plant intake to avoid potential toxins that can build up if one type of plant is consumed in excess. Sustainable foraging is critical for preserving the wilderness. Always harvest responsibly, taking only what you need and leaving plenty for wildlife and plant regeneration. Rotate your foraging areas to avoid depleting any one spot. By respecting the environment, you ensure that it continues to provide for you and future generations.

2.3 NUTRITIONAL PLANNING

Surviving in the wild demands a higher caloric intake than sedentary living. Your body requires a steady supply of carbohydrates for energy, proteins for muscle repair and maintenance, and fats for long-term energy storage. Additionally, vitamins and minerals are essential for metabolic functions and overall health.

Carbohydrates: These are your primary energy source. In the wild, carbohydrates can be found in various roots, tubers, and berries. For instance, wild yams and other edible roots are excellent sources of carbohydrates. Berries not only provide energy but also essential vitamins like vitamin C.

Proteins: Proteins are vital for muscle repair and growth, especially when you're engaging in physically demanding activities such as hiking, building shelters, and hunting. Sources of protein in the wild include game meat, fish, and insects. Squirrels, rabbits, and fish are often abundant and relatively easy to catch, providing essential amino acids.

Fats: Fats are a dense source of energy and crucial for long-term sustenance. Nuts and seeds, like acorns and sunflower seeds, are excellent sources of fats. Wild game, particularly animals with more body fat like deer, also provide essential fats.

Balancing Macronutrients

Balancing these macronutrients involves not only sourcing them but also preparing them in ways that optimize their nutritional value. For example, pairing lean meat with a carbohydrate-rich root provides a balanced meal that fuels your body effectively.

Micronutrients

Vitamins and minerals, though required in smaller quantities, are vital for your health. Leafy greens such as dandelion and nettles are rich in iron and calcium. Berries offer a good source of antioxidants and vitamins. It's important to diversify your diet to ensure you get a broad spectrum of these micronutrients.

Hydration

Water is a fundamental component of nutritional planning. Dehydration can impair your physical and cognitive functions, making it harder to survive. Always prioritize finding and purifying water. Carry a portable water filter or purification tablets, and understand the natural signs that indicate a water source, like animal tracks and lush vegetation.

Meal Planning and Foraging Strategies

Planning meals in the wild requires flexibility and a good understanding of your environment. Aim to gather and consume food that provides sustained energy throughout the day.

Morning: Start your day with a meal rich in carbohydrates and proteins. A breakfast of roasted roots or tubers combined with some lean meat or fish can provide the energy you need for the morning's activities.

Midday: A lighter meal that's easy to prepare and eat on the go works best. Nuts, seeds, and dried berries make excellent midday snacks. They are nutrient-dense and provide a good mix of fats, proteins, and carbohydrates.

Evening: Dinner should be your largest meal, as it's when you have the time to cook and need to replenish your energy reserves. A stew of game meat, roots, and greens is an excellent option. It's nutritious, hydrating, and warming.

Cooking Methods to Enhance Nutrition

Different cooking methods can affect the nutritional content of your food. Understanding how to cook your foraged and hunted items to maximize their nutritional value is essential.

Boiling: Boiling is excellent for roots and greens. It makes them more digestible and helps retain most of their nutrients. Use the boiling water as a broth to avoid losing water-soluble vitamins.

Roasting: Roasting game meat and nuts can enhance their flavor and make them easier to digest. This method also helps to kill parasites in meat, making it safer to consume.

Smoking: Smoking meat and fish not only preserves them but also adds a rich flavor. This method is particularly useful for storing food for longer periods, ensuring you have a reliable protein source.

Stewing: Stewing combines all elements—meat, vegetables, and water—into one nutritious meal. It's an efficient way to cook tougher cuts of meat and fibrous vegetables, breaking them down into tender, flavorful morsels.

Sustainable foraging is essential to ensure that the environment continues to provide for you. Rotate your foraging areas to avoid depleting any one spot. Harvest in a way that allows plants to regenerate—take only what you need and leave enough behind for the plant to continue growing and for wildlife to feed on.

Seasonal changes dramatically affect the availability of food. Understanding the seasonal patterns of plant growth and animal behavior can help you plan your foraging and hunting strategies. In spring and summer, focus on fresh greens and berries, while in autumn, nuts and roots are more abundant. Winter demands more reliance on preserved foods like dried meat and stored nuts.

Finally, energy conservation is a critical aspect of nutritional planning. The effort required to gather and prepare food should not outweigh the caloric intake the food provides. Efficiently balancing your energy expenditure with your intake ensures you remain strong and capable of surviving.

3. THERMAL REGULATION

3.1 MAINTAINING BODY HEAT

Maintaining body heat in the wilderness is not just about comfort; it's a critical survival skill that can prevent hypothermia and keep you functional in harsh conditions. Understanding how to conserve and generate heat effectively can make all the difference when temperatures drop. Here, we explore the strategies and techniques to help you stay warm and safe.

Before delving into specific methods, it's essential to understand how the body loses heat. There are four primary mechanisms: conduction, convection, radiation, and evaporation. Each plays a significant role in how you manage your body heat in the wild.

Conduction occurs when heat transfers from your body to a colder object or surface, such as the ground. **Convection** happens when heat is lost to the surrounding air or water. **Radiation** is the loss of heat in the form of infrared energy from your body to the environment. **Evaporation** takes place when sweat or moisture on your skin evaporates, carrying heat away.

Insulation and Layering

Effective insulation is your first line of defense against heat loss. Layering your clothing is a tried-and-true method to create pockets of warm air and regulate your body temperature.

1. **Base Layer**: This layer sits closest to your skin and should wick moisture away to keep you dry. Materials like merino wool or synthetic fabrics are excellent choices because they dry quickly and retain heat even when damp.

2. **Middle Layer**: Also known as the insulating layer, this traps body heat. Fleece, down, or synthetic insulations work well. This layer should be thicker to provide substantial warmth.

3. **Outer Layer**: The outermost layer protects you from wind, rain, and snow. It should be waterproof, windproof, and breathable. A good outer shell prevents the elements from penetrating your insulating layers while allowing moisture to escape.

Avoid cotton, as it retains moisture and loses its insulating properties when wet. The saying "cotton kills" is a reminder of its unsuitability in cold, wet environments.

Shelter and Sleeping Arrangements

Your shelter plays a pivotal role in maintaining body heat. Whether you're in a tent, a lean-to, or a snow cave, proper insulation and design can significantly impact your warmth.

Location: Choose a sheltered spot, ideally on higher ground away from valleys where cold air settles. Avoid windy ridges and exposed areas. Natural windbreaks like rock formations or dense trees can provide additional protection.

Insulating the Ground: The ground can quickly sap your body heat through conduction. Use a sleeping pad or a thick layer of pine boughs, leaves, or grass to insulate yourself from the cold earth. In snow, a platform made of packed snow can serve as an insulating barrier.

Sleeping Bag: Invest in a high-quality sleeping bag rated for the coldest temperatures you expect to encounter. Down bags offer excellent warmth-to-weight ratios, but synthetic bags perform better in wet conditions. Add a bivvy sack or a sleeping bag liner for extra insulation.

Clothing: Sleep in dry, clean clothes. Avoid wearing the same layers you've worn during the day, as they may be damp from sweat. A warm hat and dry socks are essential, as you lose a significant amount of heat through your head and feet.

Generating and Retaining Heat

Beyond insulation, you need to actively generate and retain heat. Your body's metabolism is a natural heat source, and keeping it fueled is essential.

Calories and Hydration: Eat high-calorie, nutrient-dense foods before sleeping to keep your metabolism active through the night. Nuts, cheese, and fatty foods are excellent choices. Stay hydrated, but avoid excessive liquid intake right before bed to minimize nocturnal trips outside your shelter.

Hot Water Bottle: Fill a durable bottle with hot water and place it at the foot of your sleeping bag. This can provide hours of warmth. Ensure the bottle is securely closed to avoid leaks.

Exercise: Light exercise before settling in can raise your body temperature. A quick set of jumping jacks or brisk walking will boost your circulation. Avoid heavy exercise, as sweating can lead to moisture buildup and subsequent cooling.

Fire and External Heat Sources

A well-managed fire can be a lifeline in cold conditions, providing warmth, cooking capabilities, and a psychological boost.

Fire Placement: Build your fire close enough to your shelter to benefit from its heat but far enough to avoid any risk of sparks causing a fire hazard. Reflector walls made of logs or rocks can direct more heat towards your shelter.

Heating Rocks: Place flat stones around your fire and let them absorb heat. Once heated, carefully move them into your shelter (using gloves or tools) to radiate warmth through the night. Be cautious with this method to avoid burns or fire hazards.

Moisture Management

Moisture is the enemy of warmth. Wet clothing, whether from sweat, rain, or snow, can rapidly lead to hypothermia. Always prioritize staying dry.

Ventilation: While your outer layer should be waterproof, it also needs to be breathable to allow sweat to escape. Use vents and zippers to regulate airflow and prevent moisture buildup inside your layers.

Drying Clothes: If your clothing does get wet, dry it as soon as possible. Utilize your fire to dry items, but be careful not to place them too close to the flames where they could catch fire or become damaged.

Sweat Control: Avoid sweating by adjusting your layers according to your activity level. If you start to feel warm, remove a layer before you begin to sweat. Once you stop moving, put your layers back on to trap the heat.

Psychological Factors

Staying warm is not just about physical measures; it's also about mental resilience. Maintaining a positive mindset and staying active can help you manage the cold more effectively.

Stay Active: Keep moving throughout the day to generate body heat. Small tasks like gathering firewood, building shelter, or even just moving around your camp can keep your blood circulating and your body warm.

Mental Fortitude: Cold can be mentally exhausting. Stay focused on tasks and keep your mind occupied. Setting small, achievable goals can help maintain morale and keep you moving.

3.2 PROTECTING YOURSELF FROM THE ELEMENTS

Protecting yourself from the elements is fundamental to survival in the wilderness. The forces of nature—wind, rain, snow, and extreme temperatures—can challenge even the most experienced survivalist. Understanding how to shield yourself effectively ensures that you stay warm, dry, and safe. This section delves into practical strategies and techniques for safeguarding against the elements, helping you maintain your body heat and overall well-being.

Wind

Wind is a powerful element that can dramatically increase heat loss through convection. Even mild winds can strip away the thin layer of warm air surrounding your body, leading to rapid cooling. Protecting yourself from the wind involves both strategic shelter placement and appropriate clothing.

When setting up camp, always look for natural windbreaks such as rock formations, dense vegetation, or fallen logs. Position your shelter on the leeward side of these barriers to minimize wind exposure. If natural windbreaks are unavailable, create your own using tarps, branches, or snow walls. Constructing a shelter that withstands wind is crucial. Lean-tos, debris huts, and snow caves can provide excellent wind protection when built correctly. Ensure that the entrance faces away from the prevailing wind direction. Reinforce your shelter with sturdy materials, and if possible, add an extra layer of insulation like leaves or pine needles to further block the wind. Your outer layer of clothing should be windproof to prevent convective heat loss. Modern fabrics such as Gore-Tex are excellent choices, as they offer both wind and water resistance while allowing moisture to escape. Always fasten zippers, cuffs, and drawstrings to seal out the wind.

Rain

Rain can be a double-edged sword in the wilderness. While it can provide much-needed water, it also presents a significant threat by soaking your clothing and gear, leading to hypothermia. Staying dry is paramount to maintaining your body heat and avoiding severe health risks.

Invest in high-quality, waterproof clothing. A good rain jacket with sealed seams and waterproof zippers is essential. Rain pants and waterproof boots complete your rainproof outfit, ensuring that water does not seep through to your base layers. Ponchos can be a versatile addition, covering both you and your backpack.

Your shelter must be waterproof to protect you from rain. Tarps are incredibly versatile and can be set up in various configurations to provide effective rain coverage. Ensure that your tarp or tent is pitched taut to prevent water pooling, and always check for leaks. If you're using a natural shelter, such as a cave or overhang, ensure that it provides adequate protection and does not channel water towards your sleeping area.

Keeping your gear dry is as important as keeping yourself dry. Use dry bags or waterproof pack liners to store your essential items. If these are not available, plastic bags can serve as an emergency measure. Elevate your gear off the ground using rocks or logs to prevent water from pooling around your belongings.

Snow

Snow presents unique challenges, from building suitable shelters to maintaining warmth. It can act as an insulator, but exposure to snow can quickly lead to wet and cold conditions that are dangerous if not managed properly.

Snow can be an excellent insulator when used correctly. Building a snow cave or a quinzee (a type of snow shelter) can provide substantial warmth. These shelters work by trapping body heat inside, creating a relatively warm environment. When constructing a snow shelter, ensure it has proper ventilation to prevent carbon monoxide buildup from your breath or a small stove.

Layering is vital in snowy conditions. Start with a moisture-wicking base layer to keep sweat away from your skin, followed by insulating layers like fleece or down. Your outer layer should be waterproof and windproof to protect against snow and wind. Avoid cotton, as it retains moisture and loses its insulating properties when wet.

Cold feet can quickly lead to hypothermia. Insulated, waterproof boots are essential in snowy conditions. Use gaiters to prevent snow from entering your boots and wear moisture-wicking socks to keep your feet dry. Carry spare socks and change them if they become damp.

Both extreme heat and cold pose significant risks in the wilderness. Adapting your strategies to the prevailing conditions is crucial for survival.

Cold Weather Strategies

In extreme cold, maintaining body heat becomes a priority. Besides proper clothing and shelter, use your body heat effectively. Stay active to generate heat, but avoid sweating by adjusting your layers. If you become too cold, perform light exercises like jumping jacks or brisk walking to boost circulation.

Hot Weather Strategies

In hot weather, the focus shifts to staying cool and hydrated. Wear light, loose-fitting clothing that covers your skin to protect from the sun and prevent heat absorption. A wide-brimmed hat provides shade and reduces the risk of sunstroke. Hydration is critical; drink water regularly and avoid strenuous activities during the hottest part of the day.

Shade and Ventilation

Create shade using tarps or natural structures to reduce sun exposure. Proper ventilation in your shelter can prevent overheating. In a tent, open the vents or doors to allow airflow. If you're using a natural shelter, ensure there is sufficient ventilation to keep the air moving and cool. Surviving the elements is not just a physical challenge but a mental one as well.

Maintaining a positive mindset and staying proactive about your protection strategies can significantly impact your overall resilience.

Stress can exacerbate the feeling of cold or heat, making it harder to manage. Practice mindfulness and stay focused on practical tasks. Building a well-structured shelter, preparing your gear, and setting small, achievable goals can help maintain your morale.

Flexibility and adaptability are crucial. Weather conditions can change rapidly, and being prepared to adjust your strategies accordingly is vital. Always have a plan B for shelter and clothing arrangements. Keep an eye on weather patterns and adapt your activities to stay safe.

3.3 USING FIRE FOR SIGNALING

The effectiveness of a signal fire begins with choosing the right location. Ideally, you want a site that is visible from multiple vantage points, including the air. Elevated positions, such as hilltops, ridges, or clearings, are optimal because they maximize the visibility of your signal.

When selecting a location, consider the following:

- **Visibility:** Ensure there are no obstructions, such as dense foliage or rocky outcrops, that could block the view of your signal.
- **Safety:** Choose a site that is safe and away from flammable materials to prevent accidental wildfires.
- **Accessibility:** The site should be easily accessible to you, allowing for regular maintenance and fueling of the fire.

Building the Signal Fire

Constructing a signal fire involves more than simply lighting a fire. It requires careful preparation and execution to ensure that the fire produces a strong, visible signal.

1. **Fire Pit:** Start by creating a fire pit. Clear a circular area of at least 10 feet in diameter, removing all flammable materials. Dig a shallow pit in the center to help contain the fire and prevent it from spreading.
2. **Fuel:** Gather a large supply of fuel. Use dry wood for the initial fire and green wood, leaves, or grass to create smoke. The smoke is what makes your signal visible from a distance during the day.

3. **Structure:** Build a teepee or log cabin structure to allow good airflow and create a strong flame. Place your dry kindling and smaller sticks at the center, gradually adding larger logs as the fire grows.

Maximizing Visibility

To maximize the visibility of your signal fire, you need to focus on both the flame and the smoke.

Creating Smoke: Smoke is crucial for daytime signaling. Once your fire is well-established, add green vegetation to create thick, white smoke. Pine boughs, leafy branches, and even fresh grass work well. Be careful not to smother the fire completely; add the green material gradually to maintain a balance between flame and smoke.

Nighttime Signals: At night, the brightness of the flames becomes more important. Use dry, resinous wood that burns brightly and for a long duration. Build multiple fires in a triangular formation or in a straight line, spaced about 100 feet apart. This configuration is universally recognized as a distress signal.

Maintaining the Signal

A signal fire requires constant attention and maintenance to remain effective. Here are some tips to ensure your signal remains visible and reliable:

- **Continuous Fueling:** Keep a steady supply of fuel close at hand. Regularly add wood to maintain a strong flame and smoke production.

- **Watch for Wind:** Wind direction can affect the dispersal of smoke. Adjust your fire and the placement of green vegetation based on wind conditions to ensure the smoke rises effectively.

- **Clear Signaling:** If you have multiple signal fires, ensure they are spaced correctly and burn at the same intensity. Consistency helps rescuers identify your signal more easily.

Enhancing the Signal with Reflective Materials

Using reflective materials can enhance the effectiveness of your signal fire, especially at night. Reflective surfaces can help increase the visibility of the firelight and make your signal stand out.

1. **Mylar Blankets:** Positioning Mylar blankets or emergency space blankets around the fire can reflect the light and create a more substantial visual signal. Hang the

blankets behind the fire to direct more light outward.

2. **Mirrors:** If you have a signal mirror, use it to reflect sunlight onto the fire, adding to its visibility during the day.

Combining Fire with Other Signaling Methods

While a signal fire is powerful, combining it with other signaling methods can improve your chances of being spotted.

1. **Signal Mirrors:** During the day, use a signal mirror to reflect sunlight toward potential rescuers. Aim the reflection towards aircraft or high points where rescuers might be looking.

2. **Whistles and Shouting:** If you hear or see potential rescuers nearby, use a whistle or shout to draw their attention to your location. The sound can carry further in certain conditions and complement the visual signal of your fire.

3. **Flagging Tape or Bright Fabrics:** Hang bright-colored materials from nearby trees or structures to create additional visual markers. These can help rescuers pinpoint your location more accurately.

Safety Considerations

Using fire for signaling is highly effective but comes with inherent risks. Always prioritize safety to prevent accidents and unintended wildfires.

1. **Fire Control:** Never leave your signal fire unattended. Assign someone to monitor the fire at all times, ensuring it remains contained and manageable.

2. **Extinguishing:** Have a plan for quickly extinguishing the fire if necessary. Keep a supply of water, sand, or dirt nearby. When extinguishing the fire, ensure it is completely out by stirring the ashes and feeling for heat.

3. **Environmental Impact:** Be mindful of the environment. Use existing fire rings if available and avoid building new fire pits unnecessarily. Leave no trace by restoring the area to its natural state once the fire is no longer needed.

Beyond its practical uses, a signal fire can have significant psychological benefits. The presence of a fire provides warmth, light, and a sense of security. It can boost morale and help maintain a positive mindset in survival situations. The act of maintaining a signal fire gives you a purposeful task, keeping you focused and engaged. This mental engagement is crucial in survival situations, helping to stave off despair and maintain hope for rescue.

BOOK 3: SHELTER AND CAMPCRAFT

1. SHELTER BUILDING

1.1 LOCATION SELECTION

Choosing the right location for your shelter is perhaps the most critical decision you'll make in a survival situation. The ideal spot can mean the difference between a restful night and a dangerous, uncomfortable ordeal. When it comes to selecting a shelter location, several factors must be carefully considered, including safety, resources, terrain, and environmental exposure.

The foremost consideration in selecting a shelter location is safety. You need to ensure that your chosen spot protects you from natural hazards and potential threats.

Stay clear of areas prone to flooding. Low-lying regions, dry riverbeds, and gullies may seem appealing, but they can become treacherous during heavy rains. Floodwaters can rise rapidly, making it crucial to find higher ground for your shelter. Equally important is avoiding areas where there is a risk of rockfalls, avalanches, or landslides. Steep hillsides and cliff bases are particularly dangerous.

Look for signs of previous rockfalls, such as scattered rocks and disturbed soil, which indicate potential danger zones.

Proximity to wildlife is another critical factor. While water sources are essential, avoid setting up your shelter too close to them, as they attract animals. Ensure your shelter is far enough from animal trails and nests to avoid unwanted encounters. Remember, most animals will avoid human presence, but it's best not to tempt fate by setting up too close to their habitats.

Choosing a location with access to essential resources can make survival significantly easier. You need to ensure that your shelter is near vital supplies without compromising safety.

Water is crucial for survival, so having a nearby water source is ideal. However, as mentioned, don't camp right next to it. A distance of at least 200 feet (approximately 60 meters) is generally safe, minimizing the risk of flooding and animal encounters while keeping water within a convenient distance. Access to firewood and materials for shelter building is also important. Look for areas with an abundance of fallen branches, dry leaves, and other natural debris. This will make it easier to construct your shelter and maintain a fire for warmth and cooking.

The terrain of your chosen location affects the comfort and stability of your shelter. An ideal spot provides a balance between natural protection and a stable, comfortable base.

Search for flat, dry ground to set up your shelter. A flat surface ensures you can sleep comfortably without rolling or sliding. Avoid areas with significant slopes, as these can lead to uncomfortable sleeping positions and potential water runoff problems. Dry ground is equally important. Damp or wet ground can sap your body heat and lead to discomfort. Look for elevated spots that are less likely to accumulate moisture. If the ground is wet, create a raised bed using logs and leaves to keep yourself dry.

Natural windbreaks can provide significant protection against wind, which is crucial for maintaining body heat and shelter stability. Look for large boulders, dense shrubs, or clusters of trees that can serve as windbreaks. Position your shelter so that the natural windbreaks block the prevailing winds, enhancing your comfort and reducing the risk of your shelter being damaged by strong gusts. Exposure to the elements can have a profound impact on your survival and comfort.

The goal is to find a location that offers protection from extreme weather conditions while providing adequate ventilation and sunlight.

Consider the position of the sun when choosing your shelter location. In cold environments, a spot that receives morning sunlight can help you warm up quickly. Conversely, in hot climates, find a location that offers shade during the peak heat of the day to prevent overheating and dehydration.

Pay attention to local weather patterns. If you expect rain, ensure your shelter location has good drainage to avoid water pooling around or inside your shelter. Avoid exposed ridges and hilltops where you could be subjected to high winds and lightning during storms. In snowy environments, stay clear of avalanche paths and areas with heavy snow accumulation.

One seasoned adventurer shared a story that underscores the importance of careful location selection. After a long day of trekking through dense forests, he hastily set up camp in what seemed like a safe, flat area near a stream. Overnight, a sudden rainstorm caused the stream to swell, flooding his camp and soaking his gear. He spent the next day drying out his equipment and finding a safer, higher ground.

Another experienced hiker recounted the benefits of choosing a location with natural windbreaks. While trekking through a mountainous region, he found a small clearing surrounded by large boulders. The wind was fierce that night, but the natural barrier provided enough protection to keep his shelter intact and him warm, illustrating how the right spot can drastically improve survival conditions.

1.2 MATERIALS AND INSULATION TECHNIQUES

Building an effective shelter in the wilderness hinges on selecting the right materials and employing insulation techniques to keep warm and protected from the elements. A well-constructed shelter not only offers physical protection but also provides psychological comfort, boosting your morale in challenging conditions. In this section, we delve into the essential materials and insulation techniques to construct a shelter that ensures your survival and comfort.

The materials you choose for your shelter significantly impact its durability, insulation properties, and overall effectiveness. Nature offers a variety of resources, and understanding how to utilize them is crucial.

Wood and Branches

Wood is the backbone of most survival shelters. It provides structural support and can be used to create frameworks, walls, and roofing. When selecting wood, prioritize dry, sturdy branches that are free from rot. Green wood can be used for structural supports but should be balanced with dry materials to ensure stability and longevity. For the framework, thicker branches and logs are ideal. Use these to form the basic structure of your shelter, whether it's a lean-to, debris hut, or A-frame. Smaller branches can be used to weave into walls or roofs, providing additional stability and wind resistance.

Leaves and Foliage

Leaves and foliage are invaluable for insulation and waterproofing. They can be layered thickly on the roof and walls of your shelter to create barriers against rain and wind. In colder environments, a dense layer of leaves can trap air, providing insulation to keep the interior warm.

When gathering leaves, look for broad, flexible leaves that can easily overlap to create a shingle effect. Pine needles and evergreen boughs are particularly effective due to their water-resistant properties.

Grass and Moss

Grass and moss are excellent for filling gaps and adding insulation. Moss, in particular, can be packed into the crevices of your shelter to reduce wind penetration and improve thermal efficiency. Grass can be used similarly, and when dry, it provides a lightweight, effective insulating layer.

Use grass to line the floor of your shelter, creating a dry, insulated base that protects against the cold ground. This technique is especially useful in damp environments where maintaining a dry sleeping area is crucial.

Insulation Techniques

Effective insulation is essential for maintaining body heat and ensuring a comfortable shelter. The goal is to trap warm air inside while keeping cold air and moisture out.

Layering for Insulation

Layering is a fundamental insulation technique. By creating multiple layers of materials, you can trap pockets of air, which act as a natural insulator. Start with a framework of sturdy branches, then layer leaves, grass, and moss to build up the walls and roof.

For the roof, begin with a base layer of larger branches to create a stable structure. Add a thick layer of leaves, followed by a final layer of smaller branches or boughs to hold everything in place. This layering approach ensures that each layer contributes to the overall insulation, keeping the interior warm and dry.

Ground Insulation

The ground can sap body heat quickly, making ground insulation critical. Begin by clearing the area of sharp objects and debris. Lay down a thick layer of dry grass, leaves, or pine needles to create a barrier between you and the cold ground. This base layer not only provides insulation but also adds comfort.

In extremely cold conditions, consider creating a raised bed. Use logs or stones to elevate a platform off the ground, then cover it with insulating materials. This technique minimizes heat loss through conduction and keeps you off the cold, damp earth.

Windbreaks and Reflectors

Natural and artificial windbreaks can significantly improve the effectiveness of your shelter. Position your shelter with its back to prevailing winds and use natural formations like rocks or dense vegetation as windbreaks.

In addition to windbreaks, reflective materials can enhance warmth. If you have a Mylar blanket or reflective tarp, position it behind your fire and facing your shelter. This setup reflects heat back towards the shelter, increasing the interior temperature.

Sealing Gaps

Even small gaps in your shelter can allow cold air and moisture to penetrate. Take the time to meticulously seal any openings using moss, grass, or mud. Pay particular attention to the roof, as this is where most heat loss occurs.

Practical Insights and Anecdotes

Experienced survivalists often share stories that highlight the importance of effective materials and insulation techniques. One such tale involves a hiker caught in an unexpected snowstorm. Using fallen pine branches and dense foliage, he quickly constructed a lean-to with a thick, layered roof. By sealing gaps with moss and creating a raised bed insulated with dry leaves, he managed to stay warm and dry through the night, illustrating the critical role of insulation.

Another story comes from a group of campers who faced heavy rain in a dense forest. They utilized large leaves from nearby plants to shingle their shelter's roof, ensuring water ran off without seeping through. This technique kept their sleeping area dry, demonstrating how resourceful use of natural materials can enhance shelter effectiveness.

1.3 LONG-TERM SHELTER CONSIDERATIONS

When planning for long-term survival in the wilderness, constructing a durable, comfortable, and safe shelter becomes paramount. Unlike temporary shelters designed for a few nights, long-term shelters need to withstand the elements over weeks or even months. This chapter explores the critical considerations and techniques for building shelters that can support extended stays, ensuring your safety and well-being in the wild.

A long-term shelter must be robust enough to withstand various weather conditions, including heavy rain, snow, and high winds. The materials and construction techniques you choose will significantly impact the shelter's durability.

Begin with a strong framework using large, sturdy logs or thick branches. These provide a solid base that can support additional weight from snow or debris without collapsing. When constructing the frame, use natural notches in the wood or lashings made from vines or cordage to secure joints firmly.

One effective method is to create an A-frame or lean-to structure. Both designs offer excellent stability and can be reinforced with crossbeams for added strength. Ensure that all joints are tightly secured to prevent movement during strong winds.

Long-term shelters must be weatherproof. For the roof, use overlapping layers of large leaves, bark, or thatch to create a shingle effect that directs water away from the shelter. Adding a final layer of branches or boughs helps hold the roofing materials in place and adds another layer of insulation.

The walls should be constructed with similar attention to detail. Use woven branches, clay, or even stones to fill gaps and prevent wind and water from penetrating the shelter. If available, a tarp or plastic sheeting can be used as an additional waterproof barrier, especially on the roof and walls most exposed to the elements. Long-term shelters need to provide more than just basic protection; they should offer a level of comfort that supports physical and mental well-being. Consider aspects like space, bedding, and organization.

Design your shelter with enough space to move around comfortably and store your supplies. Cramped quarters can lead to discomfort and reduced morale over time. An effective long-term shelter should allow you to sit up, lie down fully, and have designated areas for sleeping, cooking, and storage.

Creating a comfortable sleeping area is crucial for rest and recovery. Use dry leaves, grass, or pine needles to create a thick, insulating bed that keeps you off the cold ground. Elevate your bed with logs or rocks to improve insulation and avoid dampness.

Consider constructing a raised platform if materials and time allow. A platform bed keeps you further from the cold ground, reduces the risk of moisture, and can be more comfortable for long-term stays.

Maintaining warmth is essential, especially in colder climates. Your shelter should be designed to retain heat and provide a stable internal temperature. Effective insulation starts with the walls and roof. Use multiple layers of natural materials like moss, leaves, and grass to trap air and create a barrier against the cold. Mud or clay can be used to seal gaps and add an extra layer of insulation.

For the floor, a thick layer of dry materials helps insulate against the cold ground. If possible, add a second layer of insulation under your bed area to enhance warmth. A small, controlled fire inside or near the entrance of your shelter can provide significant warmth. Construct a safe fire pit using stones and ensure proper ventilation to avoid smoke buildup. Reflective materials like a Mylar blanket or foil can be used to direct heat back into the shelter.

A more advanced option is to build a "rocket stove" or a similar efficient heating system. These stoves burn wood more efficiently and can provide consistent heat for cooking and warmth. Ensure your shelter has adequate ventilation when using any indoor fire to prevent carbon monoxide buildup.

Living long-term in the wilderness requires careful management of resources. Your shelter should be designed with sustainability in mind, ensuring you can maintain it without depleting your surroundings. Gather materials sustainably by taking only what you need and allowing the environment to regenerate. For example, when harvesting wood, use deadfall or fallen branches instead of cutting live trees. Rotate your foraging areas to avoid overharvesting any single location.

Integrate water collection into your shelter design. Use the roof to catch rainwater, directing it into containers for drinking and cooking. This approach not only provides a sustainable water source but also reduces the time and energy spent fetching water.

Long-term shelters should include a secure area for storing food. Elevated platforms or caches keep food away from scavengers and pests. If available, use containers with tight-fitting lids to protect your supplies. In colder climates, create a cold storage area by digging into the ground to keep perishables cool.

Veteran survivalists often share experiences that highlight the importance of thoughtful shelter design. One such story involves a survival instructor who built a log cabin-style shelter using interlocking logs and a thatched roof. Over several months, this shelter provided excellent protection against harsh winter storms and heavy snowfall, proving the value of investing time and effort into a durable structure. Another account comes from a hiker who constructed a long-term shelter using a combination of natural materials and modern tools. By incorporating a small wood-burning stove and reflective insulation, he created a warm, livable space that sustained him through a challenging winter, emphasizing the benefits of integrating modern technology with traditional building methods.

2. CAMP SETUP AND MAINTENANCE

2.1 LAYOUT AND ORGANIZATION

Establishing an efficient camp layout and organization is essential for long-term survival in the wilderness. A well-structured camp not only enhances comfort and safety but also maximizes your ability to respond to changing conditions and emergencies. By thoughtfully planning the layout and maintaining an orderly environment, you can create a sustainable and livable basecamp that supports all your survival needs.

Strategic Placement of Camp Elements

The layout of your camp should be strategic, taking into account factors such as safety, resource availability, and environmental protection. Each element of your camp—shelter, fire pit, cooking area, and latrine—needs to be carefully positioned to minimize risks and enhance functionality.

Shelter Placement

Your shelter is the heart of your camp, providing protection from the elements and a place to rest. Choose a location that is flat, dry, and sheltered from the wind. Ideally, your shelter should be elevated slightly above the surrounding ground to avoid water runoff in case of rain.

Position your shelter with the entrance facing away from the prevailing wind direction to reduce exposure to cold winds. In colder climates, orient the entrance to catch the morning sun, providing natural warmth as you start your day.

Fire Pit and Cooking Area

The fire pit is crucial for warmth, cooking, and signaling. Place it at a safe distance from your shelter—typically at least 15 feet—to prevent accidental fires. The cooking area should be nearby but downwind from the shelter to avoid smoke and odors infiltrating your living space.

Build your fire pit in a clear, open space using stones to contain the fire and prevent it from spreading. Surround the area with a small, clear perimeter to reduce the risk of sparks igniting nearby vegetation. Having a designated cooking area helps keep food preparation organized and minimizes the risk of contamination.

Water Source and Latrine

Access to clean water is essential, but your water source needs to be managed carefully to prevent contamination. Locate your water collection point at least 200 feet away from the latrine area to ensure sanitation. If possible, choose a spot upstream for collecting drinking water and downstream for washing to maintain water quality.

The latrine should be positioned downhill from your main camp and water source. Dig a small pit latrine at least 200 feet away from the camp, covering waste with soil after each use to minimize odors and discourage wildlife.

Organizing Your Camp

A well-organized camp not only enhances efficiency but also contributes to morale and well-being. Proper organization helps you manage resources effectively, maintain cleanliness, and ensure safety.

Storage Solutions

Storing your gear and supplies in an orderly manner is vital for quick access and protection from the elements and wildlife. Use waterproof bags or containers to keep items dry and secure. Hanging food and scented items in a bear bag or placing them in bear-proof containers helps prevent wildlife encounters.

Create specific areas for different categories of gear. For example, keep cooking equipment near the cooking area, tools and repair kits near the shelter, and personal items in your sleeping area. Labeling containers or using color-coded bags can further enhance organization.

Cleanliness and Hygiene

Maintaining cleanliness in your camp is crucial for health and safety. Establish routines for waste disposal, cleaning cooking equipment, and personal hygiene. Regularly check and clean your shelter, removing any debris or food scraps that could attract pests.

Personal hygiene should include regular hand washing, especially before handling food. Use biodegradable soap and dispose of wastewater away from your camp and water sources.

Enhancing Camp Comfort and Safety

Small touches can significantly improve the comfort and safety of your camp, making your stay in the wilderness more enjoyable and sustainable.

Comfort Enhancements

Simple improvements can make a big difference in comfort. Create seating areas using logs or stones, and consider building a raised sleeping platform for better insulation and comfort. Use natural materials like leaves, grass, and pine needles to create softer, more comfortable surfaces.

Lighting

Adequate lighting enhances safety and usability, especially after dark. Use headlamps, lanterns, or strategically placed reflective markers to illuminate pathways and critical areas like the shelter entrance and cooking area. Solar-powered lights are a sustainable option that can provide reliable illumination.

Weather Protection

Prepare for changing weather conditions by reinforcing your shelter and creating additional windbreaks or rain covers as needed. Use tarps or extra branches to enhance protection against wind, rain, and snow. Regularly check and maintain your shelter to ensure it remains sturdy and weatherproof.

Practical Insights and Anecdotes

Experienced campers often share stories that highlight the importance of thoughtful camp layout and organization. One adventurer recounted how his meticulously organized camp allowed him to quickly find essential items during a sudden storm, illustrating the benefits of systematic storage and planning. Another story comes from a group of hikers who emphasized the value of a designated cooking area. By keeping their cooking activities separate from the sleeping area, they minimized the risk of attracting wildlife and maintained a cleaner, more hygienic camp environment.

2.2 SANITATION AND WASTE MANAGEMENT

Maintaining proper sanitation and waste management in a wilderness camp is crucial for both health and environmental sustainability. The practices you implement will not only protect you and your group from diseases but also preserve the natural beauty of the area for future visitors. This section explores effective methods for managing sanitation and waste, ensuring a clean and safe camp environment. Sanitation in a wilderness setting involves more than just personal hygiene; it encompasses the entire process of waste management, including human waste, food scraps, and general camp cleanliness. Poor sanitation can lead to contamination of water sources, attract wildlife, and create an unpleasant living environment. By establishing and following rigorous sanitation practices, you can minimize health risks and maintain a functional camp.

The proper disposal of human waste is one of the most critical aspects of camp sanitation. Inadequate disposal can lead to the spread of diseases and contamination of water sources.

Choose a site for your latrine that is at least 200 feet away from your camp, water sources, and trails. This distance helps prevent contamination and minimizes the impact on the environment. The site should be downhill from any water source to avoid runoff contamination.

A simple pit latrine is an effective solution. Dig a hole about 6-8 inches deep, which is deep enough to cover waste but shallow enough to decompose quickly. After each use, cover the waste with soil to reduce odors and discourage pests. For longer stays, a more substantial latrine with a deeper hole and a makeshift seat can be constructed for added comfort.

In some situations, especially where digging a latrine is not feasible, portable toilets or human waste disposal bags (such as Wag Bags) are a practical alternative. These contain waste securely and are designed for easy transport and disposal.

Maintaining personal hygiene is essential to prevent illness and ensure overall well-being. Frequent hand washing is vital, particularly after using the latrine, handling food, or performing any dirty tasks. Set up a hand-washing station near the latrine and cooking area. Use biodegradable soap and water, and ensure that wastewater is disposed of at least 200 feet from water sources. A small container with a spout or a portable camping sink can facilitate hand washing.

Bathing helps remove dirt, sweat, and bacteria, contributing to personal comfort and health. Use a biodegradable soap and bathe away from water sources to avoid contamination. A portable shower or a simple basin filled with water can be used for this purpose. Sponge baths are an effective alternative when water is scarce. Proper management of food waste is critical to avoid attracting wildlife and maintaining camp hygiene.

Store all food securely in bear-proof containers or by hanging it from a tree branch at least 10 feet off the ground and 4 feet away from the trunk. This practice prevents animals from accessing your food and keeps your camp safe.

Burning food scraps in your campfire is an effective way to dispose of them, but only if the fire is hot enough to ensure complete combustion. Otherwise, pack out all food waste in sealed bags. Never bury food scraps as they can attract wildlife.

Wash all cooking utensils, pots, and dishes immediately after use. Use biodegradable soap and hot water. Designate a dishwashing area away from your water source to prevent contamination. Dispose of the greywater by straining out food particles and scattering it over a wide area at least 200 feet from water sources and your camp. Keeping your camp clean reduces health risks and enhances the overall experience.

Implement a routine for daily clean-up. Clear away any trash, food scraps, and debris. Regularly inspect common areas like the cooking site and seating areas for cleanliness.

Pack out all non-biodegradable trash. Use sturdy, sealable bags to store waste until you can dispose of it properly. Never burn plastic or other harmful materials that can release toxic fumes.

Practicing Leave No Trace principles ensures that you minimize your impact on the environment.

Leave No Trace Principles

- **Plan Ahead and Prepare:** Anticipate your needs and plan for proper waste disposal.
- **Travel and Camp on Durable Surfaces:** Stick to established trails and campsites to avoid damaging vegetation.
- **Dispose of Waste Properly:** Pack out all trash and waste, and manage human waste responsibly.
- **Leave What You Find:** Preserve the natural environment by leaving rocks, plants, and other natural objects as you found them.
- **Minimize Campfire Impact:** Use established fire rings, keep fires small, and ensure they are completely extinguished before leaving.
- **Respect Wildlife:** Avoid attracting wildlife to your camp and observe animals from a distance.
- **Be Considerate of Other Visitors:** Maintain a clean and quiet camp, respecting the experience of others.

Experienced campers often emphasize the value of meticulous sanitation practices. One memorable story involves a group of hikers who meticulously managed their waste and maintained a clean camp, significantly reducing encounters with wildlife and ensuring a pleasant experience for all. Their disciplined approach to sanitation not only protected their health but also preserved the pristine condition of their campsite.

Another account comes from a seasoned survivalist who highlights the importance of a well-planned latrine. By digging a deep pit and regularly covering waste, he maintained hygiene and minimized the risk of water contamination, illustrating how thoughtful waste management can enhance long-term camp sustainability.

2.3 CAMP SECURITY MEASURES

Ensuring the security of your camp is a fundamental aspect of wilderness survival. A secure camp protects you from wildlife, deters potential intruders, and provides peace of mind, allowing you to focus on other critical survival tasks. This section explores effective strategies and measures to enhance the security of your camp, ensuring safety and stability in the wild.

The first step in camp security is choosing a location that offers natural protection and strategic advantages.

Natural Barriers

Natural barriers, such as dense vegetation, rock formations, and bodies of water, can provide significant protection against intruders and wildlife. These barriers limit access points to your camp and create a physical buffer.

When selecting your camp location, look for areas with these features. Setting up near a rock wall or within a thicket of trees can reduce visibility from a distance and make it more challenging for animals or people to approach unnoticed.

Visibility and Observation

While natural barriers are important, maintaining a balance with visibility is crucial. You should be able to observe your surroundings and spot potential threats early. Choose a location with a clear line of sight in at least one direction, allowing you to monitor any approaching dangers.

Elevated positions, such as hillsides or ridges, offer excellent vantage points. They provide a broad view of the surrounding area, making it easier to detect movement and maintain situational awareness.

Perimeter Security

Establishing a secure perimeter around your camp deters wildlife and human intruders. Various techniques can be employed to create a defined and secure boundary.

Barriers and Fencing

Create barriers using natural materials like fallen branches, thorny bushes, or piled rocks. These barriers can deter larger animals and make it more difficult for humans to approach without being detected.

For added security, consider constructing a makeshift fence around the camp. Use cordage to string between trees and hang noise-making objects like empty cans or bells. This improvised alarm system can alert you to movement and provide an early warning.

Tripwires and Alarms

Tripwires are an effective and simple security measure. Set up tripwires around the perimeter, attaching them to noise-making devices like cans, bells, or even small pieces of metal. When an intruder trips the wire, the noise alerts you to their presence.

Be mindful of the placement of tripwires to ensure they are not easily visible and are positioned at an appropriate height to be effective. Regularly check and maintain these devices to ensure they function correctly.

Securing Food and Supplies

Food security is critical, as it attracts wildlife and can be a target for theft. Properly storing and protecting your food and supplies reduces these risks.

Food Storage

Store food in bear-proof containers or use bear bags to hang food from trees. Ensure that food storage areas are at least 200 feet away from the main camp to avoid attracting animals to your sleeping area. Hang bear bags at least 10 feet off the ground and 4 feet away from the trunk to prevent bears and other wildlife from accessing them.

Securing Supplies

Keep essential supplies organized and secure. Use waterproof containers to protect against moisture and pests. Store items in a designated area within the camp, and regularly inventory your supplies to ensure nothing is missing.

Camp Cleanliness

Maintain a clean camp to avoid attracting wildlife. Dispose of food scraps properly, clean cooking utensils immediately after use, and ensure that no food residue is left behind. A clean camp is less likely to draw animals, reducing the risk of encounters.

Personal Safety Measures

Beyond securing the camp, personal safety measures ensure that you are prepared for any threats that arise.

Weapons and Tools

Keep essential weapons and tools within easy reach, both during the day and while you sleep. A knife, a sturdy stick, or even bear spray can be useful for self-defense. Practice using these tools so that you are comfortable and proficient with them in case of an emergency.

Fire as a Deterrent

Fire is one of the most effective deterrents against wildlife. A well-maintained fire can discourage animals from approaching your camp. At night, keep the fire burning, and use reflective materials to maximize its visibility. However, always ensure fire safety to prevent unintended wildfires.

Buddy System

If you are in a group, use the buddy system to enhance security. Always pair up when leaving the camp for any reason, whether to gather water, forage for food, or explore the surroundings. This practice ensures that help is available if needed and that someone is always aware of your whereabouts.

Nighttime Security

Nighttime poses unique security challenges, as visibility is reduced and the likelihood of wildlife encounters increases.

Night Watches

Implement a night watch schedule, especially in areas with known wildlife activity or human threats. Rotate duties among group members to ensure that someone is always awake and alert. Use quiet, non-intrusive communication methods to alert others if necessary.

Lighting

Use lanterns, headlamps, and campfires to provide adequate lighting around your camp. Place lights strategically to illuminate the perimeter and any potential entry points. Solar-powered lights are an excellent option, providing reliable illumination without the need for batteries.

Shelter Security

Ensure that your shelter is secure before nightfall. Check for any weaknesses or entry points that animals could exploit. If possible, construct a door or cover for the entrance to provide additional security.

Practical Insights and Anecdotes

Experienced campers and survivalists often share valuable insights into camp security. One seasoned hiker recounted an encounter with a curious bear. By maintaining a clean camp and securing food properly, the bear was discouraged and left without incident. This story underscores the importance of proactive measures in preventing wildlife encounters.

3. TOOL CRAFTING AND MAINTENANCE

3.1 IMPROVISED TOOL MAKING

In the wilderness, the ability to craft improvised tools from available materials is an invaluable skill. When you're far from modern conveniences, ingenuity and resourcefulness can make the difference between mere survival and comfortable living. This chapter delves into the art of making tools from natural resources, offering insights into the techniques and materials that can transform raw nature into essential survival gear.

Improvised tool making is more than a practical necessity; it's a testament to human creativity and adaptability. It involves seeing potential in every piece of wood, stone, or bone around you. This mindset not only empowers you to solve immediate problems but also fosters a deeper connection with the natural environment.

Imagine being stranded with no tools at your disposal. The branches around you aren't just dead wood; they are potential fishing spears, shelter frames, or fire-making bow drills. Stones become hammers, blades, or weights for trapping mechanisms. Every natural resource holds multiple possibilities, waiting to be uncovered through careful observation and a bit of creativity.

Creating effective tools involves understanding both the material properties and the specific needs of the task at hand. Here are some essential tools and the principles behind their construction.

Stone Tools

Stone tools are among the oldest human inventions, and their simplicity and effectiveness are timeless.

Hand Axe

A hand axe is an indispensable tool for cutting, chopping, and even self-defense. To make one, find a flat, sharp-edged stone. Hold the stone firmly and strike it with another rock to chip away at the edges, forming a crude but effective blade. Look for stones like flint or quartz, which fracture predictably and hold sharp edges.

Hammerstone

A hammerstone is used for shaping other tools and can be made from any hard, rounded stone. Choose a stone that fits comfortably in your hand and has enough weight to deliver forceful blows. Hammerstones are crucial for creating other stone tools and breaking open nuts or bones for food.

Wooden Tools

Wood is a versatile material for crafting tools due to its availability and workability.

Spear

A spear is useful for hunting and fishing. Select a straight, sturdy branch, about as thick as your wrist. Sharpen one end using a knife or by rubbing it against a rough stone. Harden the tip by holding it in a fire briefly, ensuring it doesn't burn but becomes more resilient. For added effectiveness, attach a sharp stone or bone tip using cordage or sinew.

Bow Drill

For fire making, a bow drill is an invaluable tool. You'll need a straight stick for the spindle, a flat piece of wood for the fireboard, a sturdy bow, and a socket. Carve a notch in the fireboard and place the spindle in it. Use the bow to rotate the spindle rapidly, creating friction that generates an ember. The process of making and using a bow drill underscores the importance of understanding both materials and technique.

Cordage

Cordage is essential for binding tools together, setting traps, or creating shelter. It can be made from various natural fibers.

Plant Fibers

Plants like milkweed, dogbane, or the inner bark of trees provide excellent fibers for cordage. Harvest the fibers by peeling them away from the plant and twisting them together to form a strong, durable rope. Practice makes perfect in cordage making, as the strength of the rope depends on the consistency and tightness of the twist.

Animal Sinew

Sinew, harvested from the tendons of animals, is another robust material for making cordage. It is incredibly strong and becomes adhesive when wet, making it ideal for securing tool components. To prepare sinew, scrape off any remaining flesh, stretch it, and let it dry. Once dried, it can be shredded into fine fibers and twisted into cordage.

Advanced Techniques and Tools

Once basic tools are mastered, you can move on to more complex creations that enhance your ability to thrive in the wild.

Fishing Tools

Crafting effective fishing tools, like hooks and nets, can provide a reliable food source. Fishhooks can be carved from bones, thorns, or hardwoods. Shape the hook with a sharp point and a barb to prevent the fish from escaping. Nets can be woven from fine cordage, using a simple overhand knot to create a mesh pattern.

Trapping Devices

Traps are critical for passive hunting. Deadfalls and snares are two common types.

Deadfall Trap

A deadfall trap uses a heavy object, such as a rock or log, to crush the prey. The key is the trigger mechanism, which can be as simple as a Y-shaped stick holding the weight in place, ready to collapse when the bait is disturbed.

Snares

Snares, made from cordage, are effective for catching small game. Set the snare along a known animal path, securing it to a sturdy anchor point. The loop of the snare should be large enough for the animal to pass through but tight enough to close quickly around it. Experienced survivalists often share stories that highlight the ingenuity required in tool making. One memorable tale involves a hiker who used the bones of a fish to fashion a set of needles and hooks, which he then used to repair his gear and catch more fish. This story illustrates the importance of seeing tools not just in their immediate context but as building blocks for further survival tasks. Another account comes from a bushcraft instructor who demonstrated how to make an entire toolkit using only a few basic materials found in the wild. By creating a hand axe, hammerstone, and cordage, he was able to construct a shelter, set traps, and start a fire—all with tools he had improvised on the spot. His experience underscores the versatility and necessity of these skills in extended survival situations.

3.2 Tool Care and Sharpening

In the wilderness, tools are invaluable allies in your quest for survival. Whether crafted from natural materials or brought with you, their maintenance and sharpness are crucial to their effectiveness and longevity. Proper care and sharpening of your tools ensure they remain functional, reliable, and safe to use. This chapter delves into the essential practices for tool care and sharpening, equipping you with the knowledge to keep your implements in peak condition.

Maintaining your tools is not just about preserving their functionality; it's about ensuring your safety and efficiency. A well-maintained tool is less likely to break or cause injury, and it performs its intended tasks with greater ease, saving you time and energy. Regular maintenance extends the lifespan of your tools, making them more dependable during extended stays in the wild.

Daily Maintenance Practices

Daily maintenance involves simple, routine tasks that keep your tools in good working order. These practices prevent minor issues from escalating into major problems.

Cleaning

After each use, clean your tools thoroughly to remove dirt, sap, and other debris. Use a cloth or a small brush to wipe down metal parts, and if necessary, rinse with water and dry immediately to prevent rust. For wooden handles, a quick wipe with a damp cloth followed by drying can keep them free from grime and moisture.

Inspection

Regularly inspect your tools for signs of wear and damage. Check for cracks in handles, loose parts, or nicks in the blades. Early detection of issues allows you to address them before they compromise the tool's functionality.

Lubrication

Metal parts benefit from regular lubrication to prevent rust and ensure smooth operation. A light coat of oil on blades, hinges, and moving parts helps maintain their condition. Natural oils, such as linseed oil for wooden handles, can prevent drying and cracking.

Sharpening Techniques

A sharp tool is essential for efficient and safe use. Whether you're working with knives, axes, or improvised stone tools, sharpening them correctly is crucial.

Knife Sharpening

A sharp knife is a versatile and indispensable tool. To maintain its edge, follow these steps:

1. **Choose the Right Sharpening Stone**: Use a whetstone, diamond stone, or ceramic stone. Begin with a coarse grit to shape the edge and move to a finer grit for honing.

2. **Angle and Technique**: Maintain a consistent angle, typically around 20 degrees, while sharpening. Draw the knife across the stone in a sweeping motion, alternating sides to ensure an even edge. For serrated knives, use a specialized rod to sharpen each tooth individually.

3. **Stropping**: After sharpening, use a leather strop to polish the edge and remove any burrs. This final step ensures a razor-sharp finish.

Axe Sharpening

Axes require a robust, sharp edge to perform heavy-duty tasks. Here's how to keep them sharp:

1. **Secure the Axe**: Clamp the axe head or stabilize it on a flat surface.

2. **Use a File**: Start with a mill file to establish the edge. File in one direction, following the curve of the blade, and maintain a consistent angle.

3. **Honing**: Use a honing stone to refine the edge. Circular motions work well for honing the convex edge of an axe.

4. **Polish**: Finish with a light polish using a strop or fine-grit sandpaper to remove any burrs and enhance sharpness.

Stone Tools

Improvised stone tools, such as hand axes or scrapers, also require maintenance to stay sharp.

1. **Retouching the Edge**: Use another stone as an abrader to flake off small pieces and maintain a sharp edge. Strike lightly along the edge to create new, sharp flakes.
2. **Regular Shaping**: Consistent shaping and flaking keep the tool effective. Pay attention to the symmetry and balance of the tool to ensure it remains practical for its intended use.

Advanced Maintenance

For tools that undergo heavy use, advanced maintenance techniques may be necessary. These practices ensure your tools remain in top condition even under demanding conditions.

Rehandling

Over time, wooden handles can crack or break. Replacing a handle requires finding a suitable piece of wood, shaping it to fit the tool head, and securing it firmly.

1. **Selecting Wood**: Choose a strong, flexible wood like hickory or ash. Avoid using green wood as it may shrink and loosen over time.
2. **Shaping**: Carve the wood to fit the tool head snugly. Use a rasp or file to achieve a precise fit.
3. **Securing**: Fit the handle into the tool head and secure it with wedges or pins. Ensure it is tightly fitted to prevent wobbling or loosening.

Blade Realignment

Occasionally, blades may become misaligned due to heavy use or impact. Realigning them ensures they cut efficiently and safely.

1. **Assessment**: Check the blade for warps or bends by laying it flat on a surface and noting any gaps.
2. **Realignment**: Gently tap the blade with a hammer to straighten it. Use a soft, flat surface to support the blade during this process.

Protective Sheaths

Creating protective sheaths for your tools prevents damage and maintains sharpness.

1. **Materials**: Use leather, fabric, or even bark to make sheaths. Leather is durable and offers excellent protection.

2. **Design**: Ensure the sheath fits snugly around the blade without being too tight. Sew or glue the edges and add a closure mechanism, such as a button or strap, to keep the tool secure.

3.3 LEVERAGING NATURAL RESOURCES

Natural resources are the building blocks of survival tools. These resources include wood, stone, bone, and plant fibers, each offering specific benefits depending on the intended use. Understanding the characteristics of these materials allows you to select the best ones for crafting durable, functional tools.

Wood

Wood is perhaps the most versatile resource in the wilderness. Different types of wood have distinct properties, making some better suited for specific tools than others.

- **Hardwoods**: Trees like oak, hickory, and maple provide dense, strong wood ideal for tools that require durability, such as handles, clubs, and frames.
- **Softwoods**: Pine and fir, while less dense, are easier to carve and shape, making them suitable for containers, spoons, and lightweight structures.
- **Green Wood vs. Dry Wood**: Green wood is flexible and can be shaped easily but may shrink and crack as it dries. Dry wood is stable and strong, ideal for long-lasting tools.

Stone

Stone tools date back to the earliest humans and remain invaluable for their durability and sharpness.

- **Flint and Chert**: These stones fracture predictably and can be shaped into sharp edges for knives, arrowheads, and scrapers.
- **Granite and Basalt**: Hard stones like these are excellent for hammerstones and grinding tools due to their durability and resistance to wear.

Bone

Bones from animals provide a lightweight, durable material that can be fashioned into various tools.

- **Long Bones**: These can be shaped into awls, needles, and fishing hooks due to their length and strength.
- **Flat Bones**: Scapulae and other flat bones can be used for scraping tools and even primitive shovels.

Plant Fibers

Plant fibers are essential for making cordage, which is crucial for binding, lashing, and creating nets.

- **Inner Bark**: Trees like cedar and basswood have fibrous inner bark that can be processed into strong, flexible cordage.
- **Grasses and Reeds**: These can be woven into baskets, mats, and other containers, providing lightweight, portable storage solutions.

Gathering and Preparing Resources

Effective tool making begins with gathering and preparing natural resources. This process involves identifying suitable materials, collecting them sustainably, and preparing them for use.

Identifying Suitable Materials

Learning to identify useful materials in the wild is a skill developed through practice and observation. Look for trees with straight, unblemished branches for handles and supports. Seek out stones with a glassy or fine-grained texture for knapping. Recognize the skeletal remains of animals, understanding which bones are most useful.

Sustainable Harvesting

Sustainability is crucial to preserving the environment and ensuring resources remain available. Harvest wood from deadfall or prune live trees sparingly to avoid long-term damage. Collect stones from areas where they are abundant, avoiding sites of cultural or ecological significance. When gathering plant fibers, take only what you need and allow the plant to continue growing.

Processing Materials

Once collected, materials often need processing to become useful tools.

- **Wood**: Strip bark, trim branches, and carve into the desired shape. For green wood, allow time to dry and cure to prevent warping.
- **Stone**: Knapping is the process of striking stone to create sharp edges. Use a hammerstone to carefully chip away at the material, shaping it into blades or points.
- **Bone**: Clean and dry bones thoroughly. Soak in water to soften if necessary, then carve with sharp tools.
- **Fibers**: Separate fibers from plants by soaking, beating, and drying them. Twist or braid into cordage, ensuring even thickness and strength.

Crafting Essential Tools

With resources prepared, you can begin crafting essential survival tools. Here are some examples of tools you can create using natural materials.

Knives and Blades

Stone blades are sharp and versatile. Select a suitable stone and shape it through knapping, creating a thin, sharp edge. Attach the blade to a wooden handle using cordage or sinew, securing it firmly. This knife can be used for cutting, skinning, and preparing food.

Spears and Fishing Gear

Spears are crucial for hunting and defense. Choose a straight, strong branch and sharpen one end. For added effectiveness, attach a stone or bone point. To make fishing gear, carve small hooks from bone or hardwood and attach them to lines made from twisted plant fibers.

Containers and Utensils

Containers can be fashioned from wood, bark, and plant fibers. Hollow out logs to create bowls or carve spoons from softwood. Weave baskets from reeds or grasses, ensuring tight, even weaves for strength and durability.

Shelter Building Tools

Tools for shelter building include hammers, saws, and digging sticks. A hammer can be made from a sturdy branch and a rounded stone lashed together. Create a saw by shaping a long, flat piece of hardwood with serrated edges. Digging sticks are straightforward, requiring only a sturdy branch with one end sharpened and fire-hardened. Seasoned survivalists often share stories that illustrate the ingenuity required in leveraging natural resources. One such tale involves a hiker who, after losing his gear in a river, fashioned a complete set of tools from the materials around him. Using stone blades, he created a new shelter, hunted for food, and even made containers for water collection. His resourcefulness highlights the potential of natural materials when understood and utilized effectively. Another story comes from a bushcraft instructor who demonstrated making fire using only natural materials. He crafted a bow drill set from wood and cordage he prepared himself, igniting a fire that provided warmth and cooking ability. This skill underscores the importance of mastering resource utilization in survival scenarios.

BOOK 4: WATER SOURCING AND PURIFICATION

1. FINDING WATER SOURCES

1.1 IDENTIFYING NATURAL WATER SOURCES

Water is the most critical resource for survival in the wilderness. Identifying natural water sources can mean the difference between life and death. The landscape around you holds clues to finding water, and understanding these signs can lead you to this vital resource. This chapter explores various methods and techniques for locating natural water sources in the wild, ensuring you stay hydrated and healthy.

Water sources in the wild can be divided into several types, each with unique characteristics. These include rivers, streams, lakes, ponds, springs, and groundwater. Recognizing these different sources and their signs is essential for successful water location.

Rivers and Streams

Rivers and streams are among the most reliable sources of water. They are often fed by rainfall, snowmelt, or springs and typically provide a continuous supply of flowing water. Moving water is usually cleaner than stagnant water, as it is less likely to harbor harmful bacteria and parasites.

Lakes and Ponds

Lakes and ponds are larger bodies of still water. While they can be excellent sources of water, it's essential to treat or filter the water before consumption, as still water is more prone to contamination from wildlife and algae.

Springs

Springs are natural outlets where groundwater flows to the surface. They are often found at the base of hills or mountains and can provide clean, fresh water. Springs are generally reliable, but it's still wise to purify the water.

Groundwater and Seepage

Groundwater can be accessed by digging or finding seepage areas where water slowly flows to the surface. These sources can be challenging to locate but are invaluable in dry regions.

Reading the Landscape for Water Clues

The natural landscape offers numerous clues that can lead you to water. Learning to read these signs is a crucial skill for any wilderness explorer.

Vegetation Indicators

Vegetation is one of the most obvious indicators of water. Look for lush, green plants, as they often indicate a nearby water source. Specific types of vegetation, such as willows, alders, and cattails, are strong indicators of water. In arid regions, green patches of grass or clusters of trees can signal groundwater presence.

Animal Behavior

Animals can be excellent guides to water. Birds, especially those that feed on aquatic life, such as ducks and herons, are often found near water sources. In the early morning and late afternoon, animals typically move towards water to drink. Following animal tracks can lead you to water, but be cautious of predators.

Insects

Insects, particularly mosquitoes and other water-loving bugs, can indicate water presence. Swarms of insects often mean that water is nearby. However, be mindful that these insects can also be found near stagnant, contaminated water.

Topographical Features

The terrain itself can guide you to water. Valleys and low-lying areas are natural water collectors. Look for indentations, gullies, or dried-up stream beds, which can lead to seasonal water sources. Rock formations, especially those that trap rainwater, are also worth exploring.

Techniques for Locating Water

Once you understand the signs, various techniques can help you pinpoint the exact location of water.

Following Drainage Patterns

Water flows downhill, so follow the natural drainage patterns of the landscape. Dry riverbeds, known as arroyos or wadis, may still have water below the surface, especially after rain. Digging in these areas can sometimes reveal hidden water.

Using Natural Indicators

In addition to vegetation and animal behavior, other natural indicators can guide you to water. For instance, in dry areas, rock crevices and hollows may contain trapped rainwater. In coastal regions, digging inland from the tideline can sometimes produce freshwater, as it seeps through the sand.

Dowsing

While controversial, dowsing or water witching is a traditional method some use to locate groundwater. This technique involves using a forked stick or metal rods to sense water underground. Though scientifically unproven, it has historical roots and can be part of a broader strategy when looking for water.

Purifying Water

No matter how clear and clean a natural water source appears, it's crucial to purify the water before drinking. Here are a few methods:

Boiling

Boiling water for at least one minute (or three minutes at higher elevations) kills most pathogens. This is the most reliable method, but it requires a heat source and a container.

Filtration

Portable water filters can remove bacteria, protozoa, and some viruses. Ensure your filter is rated for the types of contaminants you might encounter.

Chemical Treatment

Water purification tablets or drops, such as iodine or chlorine dioxide, can effectively kill pathogens. Follow the instructions carefully to ensure the water is safe to drink.

Solar Disinfection

In sunny environments, solar disinfection (SODIS) can be effective. Fill a clear plastic bottle with water and leave it in direct sunlight for at least six hours. The UV rays can kill many harmful organisms.

1.2 COLLECTION TECHNIQUES

Surface water sources, such as rivers, streams, lakes, and ponds, are often the easiest to access. However, collecting water from these sources requires careful handling to avoid contamination and maximize safety.

Direct Collection

For rivers and streams, collect water from the surface where it appears clear and free from debris. Use a container to scoop water directly. It's best to collect water upstream from where you plan to wash or bathe, and away from potential contamination sources like animal tracks or stagnant pools.

Avoiding Contamination

To reduce the risk of contamination, avoid collecting water near livestock or human activity. Look for fast-moving sections of a stream or river, as the flow helps reduce the concentration of contaminants. When collecting from lakes or ponds, go a few feet out from the shore to avoid sediment and debris that accumulate near the edge.

Using Natural Filters

If possible, create a simple natural filter. Line your container with clean cloth or use a bandana to filter out larger particles. This initial filtration step helps make the water clearer and easier to purify later.

Gathering Groundwater

Groundwater can be accessed through springs, seepage areas, or by digging. These sources often provide cleaner water than surface sources, as the ground acts as a natural filter.

Spring Water

Springs are excellent sources of clean water. Collect spring water directly from where it emerges from the ground. Place your container under the flow, ensuring it doesn't touch the ground to prevent contamination.

Seepage and Digging

In areas where water seeps from the ground, you can dig a small hole to collect it. Look for damp soil or green vegetation as indicators. Dig a shallow pit and allow the water to pool. Use a container to scoop up the water, being careful to avoid stirring up sediment.

Utilizing Plant-Based Methods

Plants can be valuable allies in water collection. Certain plants store water, while others can indicate nearby water sources.

Transpiration Bags

A transpiration bag is a simple yet effective method to collect water from plants. Choose a leafy branch from a non-toxic tree. Place a clear plastic bag over the branch, securing it tightly with a cord. The heat from the sun causes the leaves to transpire, releasing water vapor that condenses inside the bag. Collect the water by removing the bag and pouring the accumulated liquid into a container.

Collecting Morning Dew

Dew can provide a surprising amount of water. Use a cloth or sponge to collect dew from grass and leaves in the early morning. Wring the collected dew into a container. This method works best in open fields or meadows where dew forms abundantly.

Cacti and Succulents

In desert environments, certain plants like cacti store water in their tissues. Learn to identify edible cacti, such as the prickly pear. Cut open the cactus, and extract the water by squeezing the pulp or allowing it to drip into a container. Be cautious of spines and use a clean knife to avoid contamination.

Solar Still Method

A solar still is an ingenious method to distill water from the ground using solar energy. It's particularly useful in arid environments where surface water is scarce.

Setting Up a Solar Still

1. **Choose a Location**: Find a sunny spot with moist soil. Clear the area of any debris.

2. **Dig a Pit**: Dig a pit about 3 feet wide and 2 feet deep. Place a container in the center to collect the distilled water.

3. **Cover the Pit**: Stretch a clear plastic sheet over the pit, securing the edges with rocks or soil. Place a small stone in the center of the plastic to create a dip directly above the container.

4. **Condensation Process**: The sun's heat causes moisture from the soil to evaporate. The vapor condenses on the underside of the plastic sheet and drips into the container.

Advantages of Solar Stills

Solar stills can produce clean water from almost any ground source, including saltwater. They are low maintenance and can operate with minimal supervision, making them a reliable method in survival situations.

Collecting Rainwater

Rainwater is one of the purest sources of natural water and can be collected easily with the right setup.

Using Tarps and Plastic Sheets

Spread a tarp or plastic sheet to catch rainwater. Ensure it has a slight slope, directing the water into a container. Secure the edges of the tarp with rocks or stakes to prevent it from blowing away. In heavy rain, this method can yield significant amounts of water quickly.

Improvised Containers

If you don't have a tarp, use any available containers to collect rain directly. Pots, pans, and even leaves can serve as makeshift rain catchers. Place them in open areas to maximize collection.

1.3 CONSERVING WATER

Water is essential for maintaining bodily functions, regulating temperature, and enabling metabolic processes. In a survival situation, your body's demand for water increases, particularly in hot or arid environments. Conserving water not only ensures you stay hydrated longer but also reduces the frequency with which you need to seek out new water sources, saving valuable energy and minimizing exposure to potential dangers.

Conserving water requires a combination of behavioral adjustments, strategic planning, and efficient use of available resources. Here are several key strategies to help you conserve water effectively in the wild.

Rationing Water Intake

One of the simplest yet most effective ways to conserve water is to ration your intake. Drink small, measured amounts of water throughout the day rather than consuming large quantities at once. This approach helps maintain hydration levels more consistently and reduces the risk of dehydration.

Avoiding Dehydration Triggers

Certain activities and environmental factors can accelerate dehydration. Minimizing exposure to heat, avoiding strenuous activity during the hottest parts of the day, and seeking shade whenever possible are crucial steps in conserving water. Wearing light-colored, loose-fitting clothing can also help reduce sweating and conserve body fluids.

Utilizing Water-Rich Foods

Incorporating water-rich foods into your diet can supplement your water intake. Edible plants, fruits, and even certain insects can provide additional hydration. For example, consuming wild berries, succulent plants, or even fish can contribute to your overall water intake.

Techniques for Reducing Water Loss

Minimizing water loss from your body is another critical aspect of conservation. By understanding and managing how your body loses water, you can extend your water supplies.

Managing Sweat

Sweating is the body's natural cooling mechanism, but it can lead to significant water loss. To manage sweat, take the following steps:

1. **Stay Cool**: Avoid unnecessary physical exertion during peak heat. Rest in shaded areas and conduct strenuous activities during cooler parts of the day, such as early morning or late evening.

2. **Use Sun Protection**: Wear a hat, long sleeves, and apply sunscreen to reduce the direct impact of the sun on your body, thereby reducing sweat.

3. **Breathe Through Your Nose**: Breathing through your mouth can increase water loss. Train yourself to breathe through your nose, which helps conserve moisture.

Minimizing Urine Output

While it's essential to drink enough water, overhydration can lead to increased urine output, which depletes your water reserves.

1. **Monitor Intake**: Drink only as much as you need to stay hydrated. Listen to your body and avoid drinking excessively.

2. **Diet Adjustments**: Consuming a diet lower in salt can help reduce the frequency of urination. Avoid salty foods, which can increase your body's need for water.

Efficient Water Use in Daily Activities

Using water efficiently in daily activities, such as cooking, cleaning, and personal hygiene, is crucial for conservation. Here are some techniques to optimize water use.

Cooking

1. **Boil Only Necessary Amounts**: When boiling water for cooking or drinking, heat only the amount you need to minimize waste.

2. **Reuse Water**: If you've used water to cook vegetables or boil pasta, let it cool and use it for drinking (after proper purification) or other purposes, like cleaning utensils.

Cleaning and Hygiene

1. **Dry Cleaning**: Use sand or dirt to clean utensils before washing them with water. This method reduces the amount of water needed for rinsing.

2. **Wet Wipes**: Carry wet wipes for personal hygiene to reduce the need for water. Ensure they are biodegradable to minimize environmental impact.

3. **Sponge Baths**: Instead of full-body baths, use a damp cloth or sponge to clean yourself, focusing on critical areas like the face, neck, and underarms.

Storing and Protecting Your Water Supply

Proper storage and protection of your water supply are vital to ensure it remains clean and available.

Containers

1. **Use Durable Containers**: Store water in durable, sealable containers that protect against leaks and contamination. Ideally, use containers with tight-fitting lids to prevent evaporation and spillage.

2. **Multiple Containers**: If possible, store water in several smaller containers rather than one large container. This approach reduces the risk of losing your entire

supply if one container fails.

Protection from Contamination

1. **Avoid Direct Contact**: When collecting water, avoid direct contact between your hands and the water source to prevent contamination.

2. **Filter and Purify**: Always filter and purify water before storing it. Use portable water filters, purification tablets, or boil the water to eliminate pathogens.

Conserving Stored Water

1. **Use Water Sparingly**: Use the smallest amount of water necessary for each task. For example, when washing utensils, use a small amount of water and clean them efficiently.

2. **Keep Containers Sealed**: Store water containers in cool, shaded areas to reduce evaporation. Keep them sealed when not in use to maintain the purity and quantity of your supply.

2. WATER PURIFICATION

2.1 BOILING, FILTERING, AND CHEMICAL TREATMENT

Boiling Water

Boiling is one of the most reliable and accessible methods for purifying water. It effectively kills most pathogens, including bacteria, viruses, and parasites, making the water safe to drink.

The Boiling Process

To purify water by boiling, follow these steps:

1. **Collect Water**: Gather water from the cleanest source available. Use a container to scoop water from a running stream, lake, or other sources.

2. **Pre-Filter if Necessary**: If the water contains debris or sediment, pre-filter it using a cloth or bandana. This step helps remove large particles and makes the boiling process more efficient.

3. **Boil the Water**: Bring the water to a rolling boil. This means the water should have large, continuous bubbles rising to the surface. Boil the water for at least one minute at sea level. At higher elevations, where the boiling point is lower, boil for

three minutes to ensure all pathogens are killed.

Advantages of Boiling

- **Effectiveness**: Boiling is highly effective against a wide range of pathogens.
- **No Special Equipment Needed**: All you need is a heat source and a container.
- **Immediate Results**: Once boiled, the water is immediately safe to drink.

Considerations

- **Fuel Consumption**: Boiling water requires a consistent heat source, which may consume valuable fuel.
- **Cooling Time**: You need to wait for the water to cool before drinking.
- **Taste**: Boiling can leave the water with a flat taste, as dissolved oxygen is lost. To improve the taste, aerate the water by pouring it back and forth between two containers.

Filtering Water

Water filters are designed to remove contaminants, including bacteria, protozoa, and, in some cases, viruses. Portable water filters are a popular choice for backpackers, campers, and survivalists due to their convenience and efficiency.

Types of Water Filters

1. **Pump Filters**: These filters use a hand pump to force water through a filtration medium. They are effective and can filter large quantities of water quickly.
2. **Gravity Filters**: Gravity filters allow water to flow from a higher container through the filter into a lower container. They are easy to use and can filter large volumes without much effort.
3. **Straw Filters**: Personal straw filters allow you to drink directly from a water source. They are lightweight and portable, ideal for emergencies or quick hydration needs.

Using a Water Filter

1. **Assemble the Filter**: Follow the manufacturer's instructions to set up the filter correctly.
2. **Collect Water**: Gather water from your source and pre-filter if necessary to remove large particles.
3. **Filter the Water**: Use the filter as directed, either by pumping, allowing gravity to flow, or drinking directly through a straw filter.

4. **Store Clean Water**: Store the filtered water in a clean container.

Advantages of Filtering

- **Convenience**: Filters are portable and easy to use.
- **Efficiency**: Filters provide clean water quickly.
- **Taste**: Filtration often improves the taste by removing sediment and some chemicals.

Considerations

- **Maintenance**: Filters require regular cleaning and replacement of cartridges.
- **Limitations**: Not all filters remove viruses. Ensure your filter is rated for the contaminants you are concerned about.

Chemical Treatment

Chemical treatment involves using substances like iodine, chlorine, or chlorine dioxide to disinfect water. This method is lightweight, easy to carry, and effective against many pathogens.

Types of Chemical Treatments

1. **Iodine**: Iodine tablets or liquid can disinfect water but may leave a taste that some people find unpleasant.
2. **Chlorine**: Similar to household bleach, chlorine tablets or drops are effective and widely available.
3. **Chlorine Dioxide**: This chemical is highly effective against bacteria, viruses, and protozoa, and it tends to leave less of an aftertaste than iodine.

Using Chemical Treatments

1. **Collect Water**: Gather water and pre-filter if necessary.
2. **Add Chemicals**: Follow the instructions for the specific chemical treatment you are using. Typically, you add a certain number of drops or tablets per liter of water.
3. **Wait**: Allow the chemicals to work for the specified amount of time. This waiting period ensures all pathogens are killed. The time can vary but generally ranges from 30 minutes to 4 hours.

Advantages of Chemical Treatment

- **Portability**: Small and lightweight, making it ideal for carrying in a backpack or emergency kit.
- **Versatility**: Effective against a wide range of pathogens, including viruses.

Considerations

- **Taste**: Some chemicals can leave an unpleasant taste.
- **Chemical Exposure**: Long-term use of certain chemicals, like iodine, is not recommended due to potential health risks.
- **Waiting Time**: Chemical treatments require a waiting period before the water is safe to drink.

2.2 SOLAR WATER DISINFECTION

Solar water disinfection leverages the ultraviolet (UV) rays from the sun to kill pathogens in water. The process is simple yet effective: fill a transparent plastic bottle with water, place it in direct sunlight, and let the UV rays do the work. UV-A radiation, in combination with increased water temperature, effectively destroys bacteria, viruses, and parasites.

The effectiveness of solar disinfection lies in the synergy between UV-A rays and heat. UV-A rays penetrate the water and damage the DNA and RNA of microorganisms, rendering them incapable of reproduction and survival. Additionally, temperatures above 50°C (122°F) enhance the disinfection process by accelerating the inactivation of pathogens.

Factors Influencing SODIS Effectiveness

1. **Sunlight Intensity**: The process relies on sufficient sunlight. Optimal conditions are clear, sunny days with minimal cloud cover.
2. **Water Turbidity**: Clear water allows better UV penetration. Highly turbid water should be pre-filtered to remove particles.
3. **Bottle Type**: Use transparent PET plastic bottles, as these allow maximum UV-A penetration. Avoid using glass or colored bottles.
4. **Exposure Time**: Typically, 6 hours of direct sunlight is required for effective disinfection. In partially cloudy conditions, extend the exposure time to 2 days.

Steps for Implementing SODIS

1. Collecting and Pre-Filtering Water

Start by collecting water from the cleanest available source. If the water is visibly turbid, pre-filter it using a cloth, coffee filter, or similar material. This step is crucial to remove particles that can shield microorganisms from UV radiation.

2. Choosing the Right Bottle

Select transparent PET plastic bottles, which are commonly used for soda and water. These bottles are preferred because they allow UV rays to penetrate effectively. Ensure the bottles are clean and free from scratches, which can scatter UV light and reduce efficiency.

3. Filling the Bottles

Fill the bottles with pre-filtered water, leaving a small air gap at the top. This gap helps with oxygenation, which can enhance the disinfection process. Cap the bottles tightly to prevent contamination.

4. Placing the Bottles in Sunlight

Place the filled bottles in direct sunlight on a reflective surface, such as a sheet of metal or aluminum foil, to maximize UV exposure. The bottles should lie flat and not be stacked on top of each other. A sunny rooftop or open field works well.

5. Timing the Exposure

Leave the bottles in direct sunlight for at least 6 hours on a clear, sunny day. If the weather is partially cloudy, extend the exposure to 2 days. The goal is to ensure continuous exposure to UV-A rays and sufficient heat.

For areas with limited sunlight, consider using a solar reflector to concentrate UV rays onto the bottles. A simple reflector can be made from aluminum foil or a reflective emergency blanket. While SODIS is effective, it does not remove chemical contaminants or heavy metals. Always ensure that your water source is as clean as possible and consider combining SODIS with other purification methods if necessary. Regularly inspect your bottles for damage. Replace them if they become scratched or cloudy. Store the purified water in clean, covered containers to prevent recontamination.

2.3 DISTILLATION METHODS

Distillation is one of the most effective methods for purifying water in the wilderness. It involves heating water to create steam and then condensing that steam back into liquid, leaving impurities behind. This process not only removes pathogens but also separates water from salts, heavy metals, and other contaminants. Distillation can be a lifesaver in situations where water quality is highly questionable, such as in coastal areas or regions with industrial pollution.

The principle behind distillation is straightforward. By heating water, you turn it into steam, which then rises, leaving impurities behind. When this steam cools down and condenses back into water, it is much purer than the original source. This method is highly effective because most contaminants do not evaporate with the water and are left behind in the original container.

Several distillation techniques can be employed in a survival scenario. Each method has its own set of advantages and limitations, but all share the same fundamental process of evaporation and condensation.

Simple Solar Still

A solar still uses the sun's energy to purify water. It's a low-tech, passive method that can be set up with minimal materials.

1. **Dig a Pit**: Choose a sunny spot and dig a pit about three feet wide and two feet deep. Ensure the bottom of the pit is smooth.

2. **Place a Container**: Position a container in the center of the pit to collect the distilled water.

3. **Add Moisture Sources**: Fill the pit with any available sources of moisture. This could be dirty water, plant material, or even urine.

4. **Cover with Plastic**: Stretch a clear plastic sheet over the pit, securing the edges with rocks or soil. Place a small stone in the center of the plastic to create a dip, directly above the container.

5. **Condensation Process**: As the sun heats the pit, water evaporates and condenses on the underside of the plastic sheet. The droplets then run down to the lowest point and drip into the container.

Advantages:

- Uses renewable energy
- Can purify various sources of moisture
- Low-tech and easy to set up

Limitations:

- Dependent on sunny weather
- Slow process, yields limited amounts of water daily

Portable Distillation Units

Portable distillation units are more complex but can be highly effective, especially in situations where fuel is available. These units are designed to be compact and efficient.

1. **Set Up the Unit**: Follow the manufacturer's instructions to assemble the distillation unit.
2. **Heat the Water**: Fill the unit's reservoir with contaminated water and heat it using a camp stove or fire. The water will begin to evaporate.
3. **Condense the Steam**: The unit directs the steam through a cooling coil or condenser, where it turns back into liquid water.
4. **Collect the Distilled Water**: The purified water drips into a clean collection container.

Advantages:

- Efficient and can produce larger quantities of water
- Effective in a wide range of environments

Limitations:

- Requires fuel for heating
- More complex and may require maintenance

Improvised Distillation

Improvised distillation can be done with materials at hand when commercial units are not available. This method can be particularly useful in survival scenarios where you need to purify seawater or heavily contaminated sources.

1. **Set Up Two Containers**: Place one container with the contaminated water over a heat source. Use a second container to collect the distilled water.
2. **Create a Condensing Surface**: Use a piece of metal or glass as a condensing surface. Position it so that steam from the boiling water can condense on it and drip into the clean container.
3. **Heat and Condense**: Heat the contaminated water to create steam. The steam rises, hits the condensing surface, and turns back into liquid water, which then drips into the clean container.

Advantages:

- Can be set up with improvised materials
- Effective for desalination and heavy contamination

Limitations:

- Requires a reliable heat source
- Can be labor-intensive and less efficient than commercial units

While distillation is highly effective, there are practical considerations to ensure its success in the wild. Distillation, especially when using heat sources other than the sun, can be fuel-intensive. It's crucial to manage your fuel resources wisely. Plan your distillation sessions during periods when you have ample fuel and consider using efficient stoves or fire setups to conserve energy. Ensure that your distillation setup is stable and secure. Any leaks in the system can result in loss of water and efficiency. Regularly check seals, joints, and the integrity of your containers and covers to maintain optimal performance. Monitor the yield and quality of the distilled water. Although distillation is highly effective, ensure that the distilled water doesn't get recontaminated during the collection process. Use clean, sterile containers to store the purified water and keep them sealed.

3. STORING AND TRANSPORTING WATER

3.1 SAFE WATER STORAGE SOLUTIONS

Ensuring safe water storage is a critical aspect of wilderness survival. Proper storage solutions protect your water from contamination, preserve its quality, and make it easier to transport. Whether you are storing water for a few days or planning for a long-term stay in the wild, understanding the best practices and options for water storage can significantly enhance your chances of staying hydrated and healthy.

Water storage in the wilderness serves multiple purposes. It not only ensures a reliable supply of clean drinking water but also minimizes the risk of contamination and makes transportation more manageable. Without proper storage, water can become a vector for disease, leading to severe health problems.

Choosing the right container is the first step in ensuring safe water storage. Different materials and designs offer various benefits, and the choice largely depends on the availability, intended use, and duration of storage.

Plastic Containers

Plastic containers are lightweight, durable, and widely available. When selecting plastic containers, ensure they are made from food-grade, BPA-free plastic to avoid chemical leaching. Common options include:

1. **Water Bottles**: Lightweight and portable, suitable for daily hydration needs.
2. **Collapsible Containers**: These save space when empty and can hold significant volumes when filled.
3. **Jerry Cans**: Robust and capable of storing large amounts of water, ideal for base camps.

Metal Containers

Metal containers, such as stainless steel or aluminum, are highly durable and resistant to UV damage. They are suitable for long-term storage but can be heavier than plastic options.

1. **Stainless Steel Bottles**: Resistant to dents and corrosion, ideal for both storage and transport.
2. **Aluminum Canteens**: Lightweight and durable, often used by military personnel.

Glass Containers

Glass containers provide a non-reactive option that doesn't affect the taste of water. However, they are fragile and heavier than other materials, making them less ideal for rugged outdoor use.

Techniques for Safe Water Storage

Proper storage techniques ensure that your water remains clean and safe to drink over time. Here are some key practices to follow:

Sterilizing Containers

Before filling any container, sterilize it to eliminate potential contaminants. Use boiling water, chemical disinfectants, or UV sterilization to clean the interior thoroughly.

Filling Containers

When filling containers, avoid direct contact with the water source to prevent contamination. Use clean, sterile funnels or scoops, and fill the containers to the brim to minimize air space, which can harbor bacteria.

Sealing and Labeling

Seal containers tightly to prevent leaks and contamination. If storing different batches of water, label each container with the date of collection and any relevant notes about its source and treatment.

Storage Environment

Store water containers in a cool, dark place to prevent the growth of algae and bacteria. Avoid direct sunlight, which can degrade plastic containers and promote microbial growth.

Long-Term Water Storage Solutions

For extended stays in the wilderness, long-term water storage requires additional considerations to ensure safety and sustainability.

Large Capacity Containers

For long-term storage, use large capacity containers such as barrels or drums. These can store significant amounts of water and are typically made from durable, food-grade plastic.

Water Treatment

Treat stored water periodically to ensure its safety. Use chemical treatments like chlorine or iodine, or employ UV sterilization devices to maintain water quality.

Regular Inspection

Regularly inspect your stored water for signs of contamination, such as cloudiness, off-smells, or algae growth. Replace or re-treat water if any issues are detected.

Portable Water Storage Solutions

When on the move, portable water storage solutions are essential. They need to be lightweight, durable, and easy to carry.

Hydration Bladders

Hydration bladders, integrated into backpacks, offer a convenient way to carry and access water while hiking. They come with hoses for easy drinking and can hold several liters of water.

Water Pouches

Flexible water pouches are lightweight and can be folded when empty. They are suitable for short hikes or as emergency backup storage.

DIY Solutions

In survival scenarios, you may need to improvise water storage solutions. Use materials like large leaves, waterproof fabric, or even hollowed-out bamboo to create temporary containers.

3.2 PORTABLE WATER CARRYING TECHNIQUES

Transporting water efficiently and safely is a critical skill in wilderness survival. The ability to carry water over long distances, while minimizing weight and maintaining water quality, ensures that you remain hydrated during your journey. This sub-chapter explores various portable water carrying techniques, offering practical insights and strategies to help you manage this vital resource effectively.

In the wilderness, water sources can be sparse and spread out. Having the ability to carry sufficient water with you is essential for survival, especially when traveling through arid regions or on long treks where water points are far apart. Efficient water carrying techniques can make the difference between staying hydrated and facing the dangerous effects of dehydration.

Choosing the right water container is the first step in ensuring that you can transport water effectively. The ideal container should be lightweight, durable, and easy to carry. Here are some popular options:

Hydration Bladders

Hydration bladders, also known as hydration reservoirs, are flexible, lightweight pouches that fit inside a backpack. They come with a hose and a bite valve, allowing you to drink without having to stop and open a bottle.

Advantages:

- Hands-free drinking.
- Large capacity (up to 3 liters or more).
- Compact and lightweight.

Considerations:

- Requires regular cleaning to prevent mold and bacteria.
- Potential for leaks if not properly maintained.

Collapsible Water Bottles

Collapsible water bottles are made from flexible materials that can be rolled or folded when empty, saving space in your pack.

Advantages:

- Lightweight and space-saving.
- Durable and reusable.

Considerations:

- May be less durable than rigid bottles.
- Can be challenging to clean thoroughly.

Rigid Water Bottles

Traditional rigid water bottles made from plastic, stainless steel, or aluminum are reliable and widely used. They are easy to fill and clean, making them a staple for many outdoor enthusiasts.

Advantages:

- Durable and easy to clean.
- Wide mouth for easy filling and drinking.

Considerations:

- Bulkier and heavier compared to collapsible options.
- Takes up constant space in your pack.

Carrying Water Efficiently

Once you've chosen your water containers, the next step is to carry them efficiently. Proper packing and placement can make a significant difference in your comfort and balance during your journey.

Packing Techniques

1. **Distribute Weight Evenly**: Place heavy water containers close to your back and at the center of your pack. This helps maintain balance and reduces strain on your shoulders and back.

2. **Use Compression Straps**: Secure water containers with compression straps to prevent them from shifting while you move. This ensures stability and minimizes discomfort.

3. **Accessible Placement**: Keep at least one water container easily accessible, such as in a side pocket or attached to a shoulder strap. This allows you to hydrate without stopping.

Carrying Techniques

1. **Hydration Bladder**: If using a hydration bladder, place it in the designated compartment of your backpack. Route the drinking hose over your shoulder for easy access. Ensure the bladder is securely positioned to prevent sloshing.

2. **Multiple Containers**: When carrying multiple water bottles, distribute them

evenly in your pack. Consider using smaller containers to balance the load more effectively.

3. **Waist Packs and Belts**: For shorter hikes or quick access, consider using a waist pack or belt with built-in water bottle holders. This keeps your water within reach and reduces the load on your back.

Improvised Water Carrying Solutions

In survival situations, you may need to improvise water carrying solutions using available materials. Here are a few creative methods:

Plastic Bags

If you have access to sturdy plastic bags, they can serve as temporary water containers. Double-bagging helps prevent leaks. Secure the bags tightly and carry them carefully to avoid punctures.

Natural Containers

Nature provides various materials that can be used to carry water. Large leaves, hollowed-out gourds, and even bamboo sections can serve as makeshift containers. Ensure these natural containers are clean and free from harmful substances.

Tarp or Cloth

A piece of tarp or thick cloth can be fashioned into a water-carrying sling. Place the water source in the center, gather the edges, and tie them securely. Carry the sling over your shoulder or across your back for easier transport.

Ensuring Water Quality During Transport

Maintaining water quality during transport is crucial to avoid contamination. Here are some tips to ensure your water remains safe to drink:

Sealing Containers

Ensure all water containers are sealed tightly to prevent spills and contamination. Check for leaks before starting your journey.

Avoiding Contaminants

Keep water containers away from potential contaminants, such as fuel, chemicals, or dirty gear. Store water separately from other items to maintain its purity.

Regular Cleaning

Clean your water containers regularly to prevent the buildup of bacteria and mold. Use a mild soap and warm water, and let them dry completely before refilling.

3.3 MONITORING WATER QUALITY

In the wilderness, ensuring the quality of your water supply is paramount to survival. Contaminated water can lead to severe health issues, undermining your ability to navigate and thrive in challenging environments. This subchapter delves into the methods and techniques for monitoring water quality, ensuring that your stored and transported water remains safe for consumption.

The Importance of Monitoring Water Quality

Water quality monitoring is crucial for preventing waterborne diseases caused by bacteria, viruses, protozoa, and chemical contaminants. Regularly checking your water's quality can help identify potential hazards early, allowing you to take corrective measures before consumption. This vigilance not only protects your health but also provides peace of mind, enabling you to focus on other survival tasks.

Visual Inspection

The first step in monitoring water quality is a thorough visual inspection. While this method cannot detect microscopic pathogens, it can help identify visible contaminants and irregularities.

Clarity

Examine the water for clarity. Clear water is generally safer than turbid water, which can contain suspended particles, organic matter, and microorganisms. Hold the water up to the light to check for cloudiness or visible debris.

Color

Natural water sources can vary in color due to dissolved minerals and organic material. However, water that appears unusually colored—such as green, blue, or reddish—may indicate contamination from algae blooms, chemical pollutants, or rust.

Odor

Freshwater should have a neutral smell. A foul or unusual odor can indicate the presence of biological contaminants or chemicals. If the water smells like sewage, rotten eggs, or chemicals, it should not be consumed without proper treatment.

Simple Field Tests

In addition to visual inspection, simple field tests can provide more detailed information about water quality. These tests are easy to perform and require minimal equipment.

pH Testing

The pH level of water indicates its acidity or alkalinity, which can affect both its safety and taste. Water with a pH level between 6.5 and 8.5 is generally considered safe for consumption. pH test strips or portable pH meters are inexpensive tools that provide quick readings.

Turbidity Testing

Turbidity measures the cloudiness of water caused by suspended particles. High turbidity can harbor pathogens and reduce the effectiveness of disinfection methods. A turbidity tube or Secchi disk can be used to measure the clarity of the water.

Temperature Check

Water temperature can affect the growth of microorganisms. Warmer water tends to support higher bacterial activity. A simple thermometer can help monitor temperature, ensuring it remains within a safer range, particularly if the water is stored for extended periods.

Advanced Water Quality Monitoring

For a more comprehensive analysis, advanced water quality monitoring techniques can detect specific contaminants and provide a clearer picture of water safety.

Portable Water Testing Kits

Portable water testing kits are designed for field use and can test for various parameters, including coliform bacteria, nitrates, chlorine, and heavy metals. These kits often include color-coded test strips or reagents that change color in the presence of specific contaminants.

Digital Water Quality Meters

Digital meters offer precise measurements of parameters like pH, turbidity, dissolved oxygen, and conductivity. While more expensive, these devices provide accurate and reliable data, making them valuable tools for long-term expeditions.

Maintaining Water Quality During Storage and Transport

Once you have ensured that your water is clean, maintaining its quality during storage and transport is essential. Here are some best practices:

Clean Containers

Always use clean, sterilized containers for storing and transporting water. Any residual contaminants in the container can compromise water quality. Regularly clean and sanitize containers with hot water and biodegradable soap, followed by a thorough rinse.

Sealed Storage

Keep water containers tightly sealed to prevent contamination from external sources. Store containers in a cool, dark place to inhibit bacterial growth and reduce the risk of chemical leaching from plastic containers.

Avoiding Cross-Contamination

Use separate containers for treated and untreated water to prevent cross-contamination. Clearly label each container and avoid dipping used utensils into clean water.

Monitoring Water Sources

When collecting water from natural sources, regular monitoring of these sources can help ensure their continued safety.

Seasonal Changes

Water quality can fluctuate with seasonal changes. For instance, spring runoff can introduce higher levels of sediment and organic matter, while summer heat can promote algal blooms. Be aware of these changes and adjust your water collection and treatment methods accordingly.

Environmental Indicators

Monitor the surrounding environment for indicators of contamination, such as animal activity, industrial runoff, or agricultural practices. These factors can introduce pathogens and chemicals into the water supply.

Regular Testing

Even if a water source appears safe, periodic testing is crucial. Use portable testing kits or field tests to check the water quality regularly, particularly after heavy rainfall or significant environmental changes.

BOOK 5: FOOD PROCUREMENT AND STORAGE

1. HUNTING AND TRAPPING

1.1 BASIC TRAPPING TECHNIQUES

Mastering basic trapping techniques is an essential skill for any survivalist. Traps provide a reliable source of food when hunting with weapons is impractical or when conserving energy is crucial. Understanding various trapping methods, selecting the appropriate locations, and building effective traps can significantly increase your chances of securing a meal in the wilderness.

Principles of Effective Trapping

1. **Understanding Animal Behavior**:
   - **Habitat**: Identify areas where animals are likely to be found, such as near water sources, game trails, and feeding grounds.
   - **Patterns**: Observe signs of animal activity like tracks, droppings, and feeding marks to determine the best trapping locations.
   - **Bait and Lures**: Use natural baits and scents that attract specific animals,

increasing the likelihood of trapping success.

2. **Trap Placement**:

- **Strategic Locations**: Place traps in areas with high animal traffic. Natural funnels, such as trails and bottlenecks, are ideal.
- **Concealment**: Ensure traps are well-hidden to avoid detection by both animals and humans. Use natural materials to blend the traps with the surroundings.

3. **Safety and Ethics**:

- **Humane Trapping**: Aim for quick and humane kills to minimize the animal's suffering. Regularly check traps to ensure captured animals do not suffer unnecessarily.
- **Legal Considerations**: Be aware of local laws and regulations regarding trapping. Ensure your methods comply with ethical and legal standards.

Common Trapping Techniques

1. **Snare Traps**:

- **Description**: Snares are simple yet effective traps that use a noose to capture animals by the neck or leg.
- **Materials Needed**: Strong wire, cordage, or natural vines.
- **Construction**:
  - Create a loop large enough to fit the target animal's head or leg.
  - Attach the loop to a secure anchor point, such as a tree or stake.
  - Position the loop on a well-used animal trail, at the appropriate height for the target species.

2. **Deadfall Traps**:

- **Description**: Deadfall traps use a heavy object, such as a rock or log, to crush the animal.
- **Materials Needed**: Heavy object, trigger mechanism (sticks or stones), bait.
- **Construction**:
  - Set up a trigger mechanism using sticks arranged in a "figure-four" configuration.
  - Place the heavy object above the trigger setup.

- Bait the trap to lure the animal under the deadfall.

3. **Pitfall Traps**:
   - **Description**: These traps involve digging a pit and covering it with a weak support that collapses under the animal's weight.
   - **Materials Needed**: Digging tools, natural materials for covering (leaves, sticks).
   - **Construction**:
     - Dig a pit deep enough to prevent the animal from escaping.
     - Cover the pit with weak materials that blend with the surroundings.
     - Add bait inside the pit to attract the animal.

4. **Spring Traps**:
   - **Description**: Spring traps use tension (from a bent sapling or similar mechanism) to capture or kill the animal.
   - **Materials Needed**: Sapling or flexible branch, cordage, trigger mechanism.
   - **Construction**:
     - Bend a sapling or branch and secure it in place using a trigger mechanism.
     - Attach a snare or noose to the sapling.
     - Set the trigger to release the tension when the animal disturbs it.

5. **Fishing Traps**:
   - **Description**: Fish traps capture aquatic animals and can be made using simple materials.
   - **Materials Needed**: Flexible branches, cordage, bait.
   - **Construction**:
     - Create a funnel-shaped trap using flexible branches tied together.
     - Place the trap in a stream or river, with the narrow end facing downstream.
     - Bait the trap to attract fish.

Tips for Trapping Success

1. **Camouflage and Concealment**:
   - Use natural materials to hide traps effectively.
   - Avoid disturbing the area too much, which can alert animals to your

presence.

2. **Regular Maintenance and Monitoring**:
   - Check traps frequently to ensure they are in working order and to humanely deal with captured animals.
   - Reset traps as needed and replace any damaged components.

3. **Adaptability and Innovation**:
   - Be prepared to modify traps based on the materials available and the behavior of the local wildlife.
   - Combine different trapping techniques to increase the likelihood of success.

4. **Learning from Experience**:
   - Keep a journal of your trapping efforts, noting what works and what doesn't.
   - Learn from each attempt and refine your techniques accordingly.

5. **Environmental Considerations**:
   - Be mindful of the impact on the local ecosystem.
   - Avoid over-trapping in a single area to ensure sustainable use of wildlife resources.

1.2 HUNTING WITH PRIMITIVE WEAPONS

Hunting with primitive weapons is an essential survival skill that taps into the ingenuity and resilience of our ancestors. When modern tools are unavailable, knowing how to fashion and use primitive weapons can mean the difference between going hungry and securing vital sustenance. This section delves into the techniques, materials, and strategies for effective hunting with primitive weapons, ensuring that you are well-prepared to thrive in the wild.

Spears and Atlatls

Spears are among the oldest and simplest hunting tools known to humanity. To create a spear, start with a straight, sturdy branch—preferably from a hardwood like oak or hickory. Strip the bark and smooth the surface to reduce splinters. Sharpen one end to a fine point using a knife or a sharp rock. For added durability and effectiveness, harden the tip by slowly rotating it over a fire, allowing the heat to remove moisture and toughen the wood. An atlatl, or spear-thrower, increases the velocity and distance of your throw. It consists of a lever-like stick with a notch at one end to hold the spear. The atlatl acts as an extension of your arm, enabling you to throw the spear with greater force and accuracy. Crafting an atlatl requires finding a flexible yet strong piece of wood, carving a handle that fits comfortably in your hand, and creating a notch or hook for the spear. Mastering the atlatl can significantly enhance your hunting success, especially when targeting larger game.

Bows and Arrows

Constructing a bow and arrows involves more precision and skill but offers the advantage of silent, long-range hunting. Select a branch from a flexible yet strong wood, such as yew, ash, or hickory. Shape the branch into a bow by carefully carving it to achieve a gradual taper from the handle to the tips. String the bow with a durable cord made from plant fibers, sinew, or rawhide.

Arrows should be straight and balanced. Choose slender, straight branches for the shafts, ensuring they are free from knots or bends. Sharpen one end of the shaft and attach an arrowhead, which can be made from flint, bone, or metal. Secure the arrowhead with sinew or strong cordage and add fletching made from feathers to stabilize the arrow during flight. Practice is crucial to develop the skill needed for accurate and effective use of the bow and arrows.

Stone Tools and Knives

Flintknapping is the process of shaping stones into sharp tools and weapons, a critical skill for primitive hunting. Locate a suitable piece of flint, obsidian, or chert. Using a hammerstone, strike the edge of the flint to remove flakes and create a sharp edge. With practice, you can shape these flakes into arrowheads, knives, and other cutting tools.

Knives made from stone or bone are indispensable in the wilderness. A well-crafted knife can be used for a variety of tasks, from preparing game to constructing shelters. To make a stone knife, find a flat, thin piece of flint or obsidian and shape it into a blade by knapping. Attach the blade to a handle made from wood or bone, securing it with sinew or plant fibers.

Traps and Snares

Trapping complements hunting by providing a passive method of securing food. Snares are simple yet effective traps that can be set along animal trails or near water sources. Use strong wire, cordage, or natural vines to create a noose.

Attach the noose to a sturdy anchor point and position it at the appropriate height for the target animal. As the animal moves through the snare, it tightens around its neck or leg, capturing it.

Deadfall traps use a heavy object, such as a rock or log, to crush the animal. Construct a trigger mechanism using sticks arranged in a "figure-four" configuration. When the animal disturbs the trigger, the heavy object falls, killing or trapping it. Pitfall traps, on the other hand, involve digging a deep hole and covering it with weak material that collapses under the animal's weight.

Using the Environment

Understanding the environment is crucial for successful primitive hunting. Animals follow predictable patterns, often frequenting water sources, feeding areas, and game trails. Observing these patterns and identifying signs of animal activity, such as tracks and droppings, can guide your hunting strategy.

Camouflage and stealth are essential. Blend with your surroundings by using natural materials to disguise yourself and your scent. Move slowly and quietly, taking advantage of natural cover like bushes and rocks. Patience and persistence are key—successful hunting often involves long periods of waiting and watching.

Ethical and Sustainable Hunting

Hunting with primitive weapons demands a deep respect for nature and ethical considerations. Take only what you need and avoid overhunting to ensure the sustainability of wildlife populations. Always aim for quick, humane kills to minimize the animal's suffering.

Respect legal regulations and hunting seasons, which are designed to maintain ecological balance. If you are hunting in an unfamiliar area, research local laws and customs to ensure compliance. Ethical hunting not only supports conservation efforts but also honors the traditions and skills passed down through generations.

Safety and Practice

Safety is paramount when using primitive weapons. Ensure that your tools are securely crafted and handle them with care to avoid injury. Regularly inspect and maintain your weapons to ensure they remain effective and safe to use.

Practice is crucial to develop proficiency with primitive weapons. Spend time honing your skills in a controlled environment before relying on them in a survival situation.

Familiarize yourself with the feel and mechanics of each weapon, and practice hunting techniques to improve your accuracy and efficiency.

In conclusion, hunting with primitive weapons is a blend of art and science, requiring skill, patience, and a deep understanding of nature. By mastering these ancient techniques, you not only enhance your chances of survival but also connect with the rich heritage of human ingenuity. The wilderness becomes a source of sustenance and a classroom where every hunt is a lesson in resourcefulness and resilience.

1.3 FIELD DRESSING AND BUTCHERY

Field dressing and butchery are critical skills for any wilderness survivalist. Once you've successfully hunted game, the next step is to process the animal efficiently to ensure the meat is safe to consume and can be preserved for future use. This process involves not just technical know-how but also a respect for the animal and the environment. Let's dive into the practicalities and subtle nuances of turning a successful hunt into a nourishing meal. Imagine you've just taken down a deer in the forest. The air is cool, and the adrenaline of the hunt still lingers. Your first priority is to field dress the animal. This crucial step involves removing the internal organs to prevent spoilage and to start cooling the meat as quickly as possible. Time is of the essence here. The process begins by laying the animal on its back and making a careful incision from the sternum to the pelvis. Be mindful not to puncture the stomach or intestines as this can taint the meat with harmful bacteria.

With a sharp knife in hand, you start at the base of the sternum. Gently, but firmly, you slice through the skin and the thin layer of muscle beneath, exposing the abdominal cavity. The key here is precision. A steady hand and a clear mind will guide the blade around the organs, freeing them without causing damage. As you work, the forest around you hums with life, a reminder of the cycle of nature you're participating in.

Once the initial cut is made, reach into the cavity to sever the diaphragm, the thin sheet of muscle separating the chest from the abdominal organs. This allows you to access the heart and lungs, which you can remove by cutting through the connective tissues. Carefully extract the digestive organs, starting with the stomach and intestines, and move them away from the body. Take care to avoid any spillage, as you want to keep the meat as clean as possible.

With the organs removed, you turn the animal over to let any remaining blood drain out. This step not only helps in preserving the meat but also lightens the load if you need to carry the carcass back to your camp. In some cultures, specific organs are considered delicacies or have traditional uses. Knowing which parts to keep and how to store them can add variety and nutrition to your meals.

Now that the animal is field dressed, it's time to move on to butchery. This task can be daunting, but with practice, it becomes an art form. Picture yourself back at your campsite, the fire crackling nearby, and the tools of butchery laid out before you: a sturdy knife, a saw, and perhaps an axe. You'll need a clean, flat surface to work on— improvised from a large rock, a fallen tree, or even a stretched tarp.

Start by skinning the animal. Make cuts around the legs and down the spine, peeling the hide away from the muscle. The hide can be used for various purposes, from making clothing to creating shelter, so take care to keep it intact. As you peel back the skin, you'll reveal the muscle groups beneath. These natural lines guide your knife as you begin the butchery process.

Begin with the large muscle groups, the quarters. These are the hind legs and the shoulders, which provide the bulk of the meat. Remove each quarter by cutting through the joints, following the natural seams in the muscle. As you work, you notice the difference in texture and density of the various cuts, a reminder of the animal's life and strength.

Next, move to the backstraps, the long muscles running along either side of the spine. These are prized cuts, tender and flavorful. With careful incisions, free the backstraps from the ribs and vertebrae. The ribs themselves can be sawed off and split into manageable sections. They might not provide as much meat, but what they do have is rich and marbled with fat.

The final step is processing the smaller cuts: the neck, the flank, and the organs you've decided to keep. Each piece is trimmed of excess fat and sinew, then divided into portions suitable for cooking or preservation. If you're planning to dry or smoke the meat, slice it into thin strips. These methods not only extend the shelf life of your catch but also intensify the flavors, making for a satisfying meal after a long day in the wild.

Throughout this process, cleanliness is paramount. Keeping your tools and workspace clean minimizes the risk of contamination and spoilage. Regularly sharpen your knife to ensure smooth, precise cuts, reducing waste and making the job easier on your hands.

As you stand back and survey your work, the satisfaction of self-reliance washes over you. The meat is neatly portioned, ready for cooking or preserving. You've honored the animal by utilizing as much of it as possible, a practice that not only respects nature but also maximizes your resources.

Field dressing and butchery may seem daunting at first, but with each hunt, your confidence grows. The forest is your mentor, teaching you through experience. Each successful butchery session enhances your survival skills, ensuring you are prepared to thrive in the wilderness. This knowledge, passed down through generations, connects you to the primal rhythms of the earth, grounding you in the essential cycle of life, death, and renewal.

2. FISHING AND FORAGING

2.1 FRESHWATER FISHING METHODS

Fishing in freshwater environments is an essential survival skill, offering a reliable source of protein and nutrients. Mastering various freshwater fishing methods can significantly increase your chances of success, turning lakes, rivers, and streams into bountiful food sources. Here, we explore several effective techniques, from simple hand tools to more elaborate traps, providing a comprehensive guide to freshwater fishing.

Hand Fishing and Spearfishing

Hand fishing, also known as noodling, is one of the most primitive and direct methods. It involves using your bare hands to catch fish, typically catfish, by feeling for them in shallow waters or holes along riverbanks. While it requires patience and a good sense of touch, hand fishing can be highly effective in the right conditions. Always exercise caution, as some fish or other aquatic animals can bite or sting.

Spearfishing is another ancient method that can be both challenging and rewarding. Using a spear, often fashioned from a long stick with a sharpened end or barbs, you wade into shallow waters where fish are visible. Standing still and waiting for the right moment is crucial. With a quick thrust, you aim to impale the fish. This method requires good hand-eye coordination and practice but can be very effective in clear, shallow waters.

Fishing with a Rod and Line

Using a rod and line is a more conventional approach and can be adapted with minimal resources. A simple fishing rod can be crafted from a flexible branch, with fishing line or strong cordage and a hook fashioned from bone, metal, or even a thorn.

1. **Choosing the Right Spot**:
   - Fish tend to congregate in certain areas like under overhanging branches, near rocks, or in shaded regions where they find food and shelter.
   - Look for signs of fish activity, such as splashes, ripples, or fish jumping out of the water.

2. **Bait and Lures**:
   - Natural baits, such as worms, insects, or small fish, are effective and readily available in most environments.
   - Experiment with different baits to see what attracts the local fish.

3. **Casting and Retrieving**:
   - Casting involves throwing the baited line into the water and letting it sink to the desired depth.
   - Once the line is in the water, you can either let it sit and wait for a bite or slowly retrieve it to mimic the movement of prey.

Traps and Nets

Fishing traps and nets are passive methods that allow you to catch fish without constant attention, making them ideal for survival situations where you need to multitask.

1. **Fish Traps**:
   - **Basket Traps**: These are typically woven from flexible branches or reeds into a funnel shape. Fish swim in but cannot swim out, making them an effective tool for catching multiple fish at once.
   - **Rock Corrals**: Construct a corral with rocks in a shallow area, guiding fish into a small space where they can be easily caught by hand or with a net.

2. **Gill Nets**:
   - A gill net is set in the water where fish are known to swim. The fish get caught by their gills when they attempt to swim through the net's openings.
   - Make sure to check the net frequently to remove caught fish and reset the net.

Using Improvised Materials

In a survival situation, you may not have traditional fishing gear. Improvisation becomes key to success.

1. **Hooks and Lines**:
   - **Hooks**: Create hooks from bones, thorns, or bent pieces of metal. Ensure they are sharp and have a barb to prevent the fish from escaping.
   - **Lines**: Use strong, flexible cordage made from plant fibers, sinew, or even strands of clothing.
2. **Floats and Weights**:
   - **Floats**: Use pieces of wood, bark, or other buoyant materials to keep your bait at the desired depth.
   - **Weights**: Small stones or pieces of metal can serve as weights to sink your bait to the right level.

Environmental Considerations

Respecting the environment is crucial while fishing. Overfishing can deplete fish populations and disrupt the ecosystem. Always fish sustainably:

1. **Take Only What You Need**:
   - Avoid catching more fish than you can consume or preserve.
   - Release smaller fish to allow them to grow and reproduce.
2. **Avoid Polluting Waterways**:
   - Do not discard waste, bait packaging, or fishing line in the water.
   - Clean up after yourself to maintain the natural habitat for future use.

Safety and Ethical Practices

Safety should always be a priority when fishing, particularly in unfamiliar or potentially hazardous environments.

1. **Be Aware of Wildlife**:
   - Freshwater habitats can host various wildlife, some of which may be

dangerous.

- Exercise caution around snakes, alligators, or other potentially aggressive animals.

2. **First Aid Preparedness**:

- Have basic first aid supplies handy to treat minor injuries like cuts or punctures.
- Be knowledgeable about treating fish bites or stings, which can happen while handling catches.

3. **Legal and Ethical Fishing**:

- Familiarize yourself with local regulations regarding fishing seasons, sizes, and protected species.
- Adhere to ethical fishing practices to ensure the sustainability of fish populations.

Fishing in freshwater environments, when done with skill and respect, provides a sustainable and rewarding way to secure food. Mastering these methods not only increases your chances of survival but also deepens your connection with nature, honing your instincts and abilities as a true outdoorsman.

2.2 IDENTIFYING EDIBLE PLANTS

Foraging for edible plants is an indispensable skill in wilderness survival. The ability to identify and safely consume wild plants can significantly extend your food resources and provide essential nutrients that are otherwise hard to obtain. Knowledge of edible plants not only enriches your survival diet but also connects you deeply with the natural world, fostering a sense of self-reliance and confidence.

The first rule of foraging is safety. Never consume a plant unless you are absolutely certain of its identity. Many edible plants have toxic look-alikes, so careful identification is crucial. Always cross-reference multiple sources and, if possible, consult with local experts. Remember, when in doubt, leave it out.

Basic Principles of Plant Identification

1. **Understand Plant Anatomy**:

- Learn the basic parts of a plant: roots, stems, leaves, flowers, and fruits. Recognizing these parts helps in accurate identification.

- Note the leaf shape, arrangement, and margins. Are the leaves opposite, alternate, or whorled? Are they serrated, lobed, or smooth-edged?

2. **Habitat and Seasonality**:
   - Identify plants in their natural habitat. Different plants thrive in different environments such as forests, meadows, or wetlands.
   - Be aware of the growing season of each plant. Some are available year-round, while others have specific seasons.

3. **Use a Field Guide**:
   - A reliable field guide with detailed photographs and descriptions is invaluable. Use it to compare and confirm plant features.

Common Edible Plants

1. **Dandelion (Taraxacum officinale)**:
   - **Identification**: Dandelions have deeply toothed leaves that grow in a basal rosette. The flowers are bright yellow and turn into fluffy seed heads.
   - **Habitat**: Commonly found in lawns, meadows, and along roadsides.
   - **Edibility**: All parts are edible. The leaves can be eaten raw or cooked, the flowers can be used in salads or fried, and the roots can be roasted and used as a coffee substitute.

2. **Plantain (Plantago spp.)**:
   - **Identification**: Broad, oval leaves with parallel veins and long, slender flower spikes.
   - **Habitat**: Found in lawns, gardens, and disturbed areas.
   - **Edibility**: The young leaves can be eaten raw, older leaves are better cooked. The seeds can be ground into flour.

3. **Cattail (Typha spp.)**:
   - **Identification**: Tall plants with long, strap-like leaves and distinctive brown, sausage-shaped flower spikes.
   - **Habitat**: Found in wetlands, marshes, and along the edges of ponds and lakes.
   - **Edibility**: The young shoots can be eaten raw or cooked. The pollen can be used as flour, and the rhizomes can be cooked or dried and ground into flour.

The Universal Edibility Test

When you are uncertain about a plant but believe it may be edible, you can perform the Universal Edibility Test. This method involves several steps to test for possible reactions and ensure safety:

1. **Separate the Plant**: Divide the plant into its basic components: leaves, stems, roots, buds, and flowers.

2. **Smell Test**: Smell the plant parts. If it has a strong, unpleasant odor, it may be toxic.

3. **Skin Contact**: Rub a small part of the plant on your inner forearm. Wait for 15 minutes. If there's no reaction, proceed.

4. **Lip Contact**: Touch a small part of the plant to your lips to test for burning or itching. Wait 15 minutes.

5. **Taste Test**: Place a small piece of the plant on your tongue for 15 minutes without chewing. If no adverse effects occur, chew the piece and hold it in your mouth for 15 minutes, but do not swallow.

6. **Swallow Test**: If no reactions occur, swallow the small piece. Wait for 8 hours. If there are no ill effects, you can consider the plant part safe to eat in small quantities.

Tips for Safe Foraging

1. **Avoid Polluted Areas**:
   - Do not forage near roadsides, industrial areas, or fields treated with pesticides and herbicides. Plants in these areas can absorb harmful chemicals.

2. **Respect Nature**:
   - Forage sustainably. Take only what you need and avoid damaging the plants. Leave enough for wildlife and for the plants to continue growing.

3. **Know the Look-Alikes**:
   - Familiarize yourself with poisonous plants that resemble edible ones. For example, Queen Anne's Lace (wild carrot) looks similar to Poison Hemlock, a deadly plant.

Foraging provides not just nutrition but also a rich sense of connection to the land. The process of identifying and gathering wild plants involves a deep engagement with your surroundings, honing your observational skills and expanding your knowledge of the natural world. Each plant tells a story, rooted in the soil of its environment, and foraging allows you to become part of that narrative.

Moreover, edible wild plants often contain higher levels of vitamins and minerals compared to cultivated varieties. They can be a vital source of nutrients, especially in a survival situation where maintaining health and energy is critical.

2.3 FORAGING ETHICS AND SAFETY

The first principle of ethical foraging is respect for nature. This respect manifests in several ways, starting with taking only what you need. Overharvesting can deplete plant populations and disrupt the local ecosystem. By limiting your take, you ensure that the plants continue to thrive and reproduce, providing for future foragers and wildlife alike.

In practice, this means leaving enough plants behind so that they can regenerate. If you're foraging for mushrooms, take care to leave some behind to release spores. When gathering berries, pick selectively, allowing some to remain for birds and other animals that rely on them.

As you forage, be mindful of the impact you're having on the landscape. Tread lightly to avoid trampling delicate plants and causing soil erosion. Use established trails where possible to minimize your footprint. If you need to venture off-trail, walk on durable surfaces like rocks or fallen logs.

Accurate identification is crucial for safe and ethical foraging. Many edible plants have toxic look-alikes, and misidentification can lead to serious health risks. Invest time in learning about the local flora, studying field guides, and perhaps even taking courses or going on guided foraging walks with experts.

One memorable foraging trip comes to mind, where I encountered a cluster of what appeared to be wild parsnips. Confidently, I began to gather them, only to pause and consult my field guide. To my surprise, they were not parsnips but water hemlock, one of the most poisonous plants in North America. This experience reinforced the importance of thorough identification and caution.

Always cross-reference multiple sources and, if in doubt, err on the side of caution. The thrill of discovering new edibles should never override the necessity of safety.

Understanding the seasonal availability of plants is another key aspect of ethical foraging. Many plants are only available during specific times of the year, and harvesting them out of season can harm their growth cycles. For example, some wild greens are best gathered in spring when they are young and tender, while fruits and nuts are typically harvested in late summer and fall.

Seasonal foraging also ensures that you're getting the plants at their peak nutritional value. Early in the season, the tender shoots of stinging nettles are packed with vitamins and minerals, but later in the season, the leaves become tough and less palatable.

Foraging can be immensely rewarding, but it's not without risks. Ensuring your safety involves several key practices. First and foremost, never eat anything unless you are absolutely certain of its identification and edibility. As a rule, always perform the Universal Edibility Test when trying a new plant, and introduce new foods to your diet gradually to monitor for any adverse reactions. Another critical aspect of safety is avoiding areas that may be contaminated with pollutants. Plants near busy roads, industrial sites, or sprayed fields can absorb harmful chemicals. Seek out pristine environments, away from human-made toxins, to gather your wild foods. Hydration and preparation are also vital. Carry sufficient water, especially if you're foraging in hot weather or remote areas. Wear appropriate clothing to protect against insects, thorns, and sun exposure. Long sleeves, sturdy boots, and a hat can go a long way in keeping you comfortable and safe. Foraging laws vary by region, so it's essential to familiarize yourself with local regulations. In some areas, foraging is restricted to certain times of the year or specific locations to protect endangered species or fragile habitats. National parks, wildlife reserves, and private lands often have strict rules about gathering plants and fungi. For example, during a foraging trip in the Pacific Northwest, I encountered a lush forest abundant with chanterelles. However, I knew that the area was part of a protected reserve, where foraging was prohibited. Respecting these regulations is crucial, as they are in place to preserve biodiversity and ensure the sustainability of the ecosystem. Ethical foraging is about more than just following rules—it's about cultivating a mindset of stewardship and gratitude. As you gather wild foods, take a moment to appreciate the environment and the resources it provides. This mindset not only enriches your foraging experience but also fosters a deeper connection with nature. Consider sharing your knowledge and experiences with others. Teaching friends and family about ethical foraging practices helps spread awareness and ensures that these practices are passed down through generations. Join local foraging groups or online communities to learn from others and share your own insights. Practicing sustainability means thinking long-term. When you forage, you are part of a delicate balance. Every plant you harvest, every footprint you leave, contributes to the larger ecological picture. By foraging sustainably, you help maintain this balance for future generations. Rotate your foraging areas to prevent overharvesting in one spot. This practice allows plant populations to recover and reduces the impact on the environment.

3. FOOD PRESERVATION

3.1 SMOKING AND CURING MEAT

Smoking meat involves exposing it to smoke from burning wood, which not only dehydrates the meat but also infuses it with a distinctive smoky flavor. There are two primary types of smoking: cold smoking and hot smoking, each with its specific purpose and technique.

Hot Smoking: Hot smoking cooks the meat while smoking it, typically at temperatures between 165°F and 185°F. This method is ideal for preparing meat that will be consumed relatively soon. To begin, you'll need a smoker or a makeshift setup. In the wilderness, you can create a smoker using a pit dug into the ground, covered with branches and leaves, and a framework to suspend the meat.

Start by selecting the right wood. Hardwood varieties such as oak, hickory, and maple are excellent choices because they burn slowly and impart robust flavors. Avoid softwoods like pine, which can produce a bitter taste and harmful residues.

Prepare the meat by trimming excess fat, which can cause flare-ups and uneven smoking. Season it with salt, herbs, and spices to enhance the flavor. Once the smoker reaches the desired temperature, hang or lay the meat inside, ensuring it's not directly over the fire to prevent charring. The key is to maintain a steady temperature and airflow, allowing the smoke to envelop the meat and cook it slowly over several hours.

As the hours pass, you can feel the transformation. The meat gradually takes on a deep, mahogany hue, and the rich aroma of wood smoke fills the air. Periodically check the smoker to maintain consistent heat and smoke levels, adjusting as needed. The process requires patience and attention, but the reward is tender, flavorful meat that's ready to eat or store for later use.

Cold Smoking: Cold smoking, on the other hand, occurs at lower temperatures, typically between 68°F and 86°F. This method is used primarily for flavoring and preserving rather than cooking, and it requires a longer duration, sometimes several days. The challenge with cold smoking is keeping the temperature low enough to avoid cooking the meat while still producing sufficient smoke.

To cold smoke, you'll need a smoker setup that allows the smoke to cool before it reaches the meat. This can be achieved by using a longer smoke path or a separate smoke chamber connected by a pipe. The goal is to expose the meat to smoke continuously, ensuring it absorbs the flavor and begins the preservation process without cooking.

Once the meat is prepared and seasoned, place it in the smoker and let the smoke work its magic. Cold smoking requires more time and vigilance to ensure the meat remains in the safe temperature range. The result, however, is a product with an intense smoky flavor and extended shelf life, perfect for long-term storage or enhancing other dishes.

Curing Meat

Curing meat is another ancient preservation technique that involves applying salt, and sometimes sugar and nitrates, to draw out moisture and inhibit bacterial growth. This method not only preserves the meat but also intensifies its flavor.

Dry Curing: Dry curing involves rubbing the meat with a mixture of salt and spices, then allowing it to rest in a cool, dry place. To begin, generously coat the meat with the curing mixture, ensuring every surface is covered. Place the meat on a rack or hang it to allow air circulation.

Over the next several days to weeks, the salt will draw out moisture, creating an inhospitable environment for bacteria. Check the meat periodically, reapplying the curing mixture if necessary. The longer the meat cures, the firmer and more flavorful it becomes.

Wet Curing: Wet curing, or brining, involves soaking the meat in a solution of water, salt, and spices. This method is faster than dry curing and can produce a more uniformly cured product. Prepare a brine by dissolving salt and sugar in water, then adding herbs and spices to your taste. Submerge the meat in the brine, ensuring it's completely covered.

Refrigerate the brining meat for several days, allowing the solution to penetrate deeply. After the curing period, rinse the meat thoroughly to remove excess salt. Wet-cured meat can be smoked for added flavor and preservation, combining the benefits of both methods.

Combining Smoking and Curing

For the ultimate in meat preservation, combine curing with smoking. Start by curing the meat using either the dry or wet method. Once cured, the meat can be smoked to add flavor and further extend its shelf life. This dual approach creates a product that is both delicious and durable, ideal for survival situations.

As you engage in the smoking and curing process, you'll find it to be a blend of science and art. Precision in temperature and timing is crucial, but so is the intuition that comes from experience. The smell of smoke, the tactile feel of the meat, and the visual cues all guide you towards a successful preservation.

In the wild, these skills can mean the difference between a fleeting bounty and a sustainable food supply. Each step, from selecting the wood to seasoning the meat, is an act of transformation, turning fresh game into a source of nourishment that can sustain you through challenging times.

As you sit by the smoker, watching the tendrils of smoke curl into the air, you're not just preserving meat—you're preserving a tradition. These methods connect you to the past, to the hunters and gatherers who mastered these techniques out of necessity. Through smoking and curing, you become part of this lineage, ensuring that the knowledge and skills endure.

3.2 DRYING AND FERMENTING PLANTS

Drying is one of the simplest and most effective methods for preserving plants. It involves removing moisture, which inhibits the growth of bacteria and mold, thereby extending the shelf life of the food.

Natural Air Drying: Imagine a sunny, breezy day as you set up your drying station. Select a well-ventilated spot away from direct sunlight, which can degrade the nutrients in the plants. You spread out your wild greens and herbs on a clean cloth or hang them in small bunches from a line. The gentle breeze and ambient warmth slowly wick away the moisture, leaving the plants crisp and dry.

Air drying works best for herbs and leafy greens. The process can take several days to a week, depending on the humidity and temperature. The key is patience—allow the plants to dry thoroughly to ensure they are well-preserved. Once dried, these plants can be crumbled and stored in airtight containers, ready to add flavor and nutrition to your meals.

Using a Dehydrator: In more controlled environments, a dehydrator can speed up the drying process. This device uses low heat and consistent airflow to remove moisture from plants efficiently. Set the dehydrator to a low temperature, around 95°F to 115°F, to preserve the delicate flavors and nutrients. Spread the plants evenly on the trays, ensuring they are not overlapping. Check them periodically until they reach the desired dryness, crisp and breakable.

Solar Drying: For those relying on natural methods, solar drying is another viable option. Create a simple solar dryer using a wooden frame covered with fine mesh or cheesecloth. Place the plants on the mesh and cover them with another layer to keep insects away. Position the dryer in a sunny spot, ensuring good airflow. The sun's heat will gradually dry the plants, while the mesh protects them from pests.

Fermenting Plants

Fermentation is a transformative preservation method that not only extends the shelf life of plants but also enhances their nutritional profile and flavor. Through the action of beneficial bacteria, fermentation breaks down plant sugars and produces lactic acid, which acts as a natural preservative.

Wild Fermentation: Wild fermentation relies on naturally occurring bacteria present on the plants and in the environment. Picture yourself preparing a batch of wild garlic and dandelion greens for fermentation. You start by washing the greens thoroughly and then chopping them into small pieces. In a large bowl, you massage the greens with salt until they release their juices. This brine is crucial for fermentation, creating an anaerobic environment where beneficial bacteria thrive.

Next, you pack the salted greens tightly into a jar, ensuring they are submerged in their own brine. Cover the jar with a cloth or a loosely fitted lid to allow gases to escape while keeping contaminants out. Over the next few days to weeks, the natural bacteria will ferment the greens, transforming them into tangy, nutrient-rich preserves. The key to successful fermentation is monitoring the process—check the jars daily, pressing the greens down to keep them submerged and skimming off any mold that might form on the surface.

Benefits of Fermentation: Fermentation not only preserves plants but also enhances their digestibility and nutritional value. The process increases levels of vitamins, such as B vitamins and vitamin K, and produces beneficial probiotics that support gut health. Fermented foods have a complex, tangy flavor that can add depth to your diet in the wilderness.

Safety Considerations: While fermenting plants, maintaining a clean environment is crucial to prevent harmful bacteria from contaminating the food. Use clean utensils, jars, and hands when handling the plants. If you notice any foul odors, slimy textures, or significant mold growth, discard the batch and start anew. Trust your senses—properly fermented plants should have a pleasant, tangy aroma and firm texture.

To maximize the longevity and utility of your preserved plants, consider combining drying and fermenting. Dried herbs can be added to fermenting vegetables to enhance flavor and nutritional content. Alternatively, fermented plants can be dried after fermentation to create portable, long-lasting snacks that retain the benefits of both preservation methods.

3.3 CREATING A CACHE

Creating a cache is a time-honored strategy for ensuring survival in the wilderness, allowing you to store food and essential supplies in a hidden and secure location. This method not only provides a safety net during emergencies but also enables you to move freely without carrying all your provisions. The process of establishing a cache involves careful planning, knowledge of preservation techniques, and an understanding of the environment.

Imagine you are deep in the backcountry, far from civilization, with only your skills and wits to rely on. You've been successful in hunting and foraging, amassing a significant amount of food. But carrying it all with you is impractical and risky. Creating a cache becomes your solution, a way to store surplus provisions safely until you need them.

The first step in creating a cache is selecting an appropriate location. This involves a blend of strategic thinking and understanding the landscape. You want a spot that is both accessible and discreet. Look for natural landmarks that are easy to remember but not obvious to others, such as a distinctive rock formation, a large tree, or a hidden hollow. The location should be far enough from common trails to avoid accidental discovery but close enough for you to reach in a time of need.

Consider the environmental conditions of your chosen spot. Avoid low-lying areas prone to flooding, as well as places where soil erosion could expose your cache. Elevation can be your ally; a higher ground might offer better drainage and reduce the risk of water damage.

With the location selected, the next step is preparing your cache. The goal is to protect your supplies from the elements, animals, and potential human discovery. Start by digging a hole deep enough to accommodate your provisions. Aim for a depth of at least three feet to ensure it's well concealed and insulated from temperature extremes.

Line the bottom and sides of the hole with natural materials such as leaves, grass, or moss. This layer provides insulation and helps protect your supplies from moisture. For added security, consider placing a wooden plank or flat stones at the bottom to create a barrier against ground moisture.

The way you package your supplies is crucial to maintaining their integrity over time. Use durable, airtight containers to keep moisture and pests at bay. Plastic or metal containers with tight-fitting lids are ideal. If these are not available, you can improvise with sturdy bags sealed with wax or tar.

Before sealing your containers, wrap each item in additional layers of protection. Cloth, paper, or leaves can be used to cushion and absorb any excess moisture.

Vacuum sealing, if possible, is an excellent method to extend the shelf life of your dried or cured foods.

Once your supplies are securely packaged, it's time to bury the cache. Place the containers in the hole and cover them with a layer of insulating material, such as more leaves or grass. Then, fill the hole with the soil you initially dug up, packing it down firmly to eliminate air pockets and deter animals from digging.

The final step is camouflaging the site. Spread natural debris, like leaves, branches, and rocks, over the freshly turned earth to blend it seamlessly with the surrounding landscape. The goal is to make the area look undisturbed, avoiding any signs that might attract unwanted attention.

As discreet as you need your cache to be, it's equally important that you can find it again. Create a mental map using natural landmarks as guides. Avoid obvious markers that could be easily noticed by others. Instead, use subtle signs that only you would recognize, such as an arrangement of stones or a specific scratch on a tree trunk. It's wise to memorize the general area and key points leading to your cache. Additionally, consider making a small, encoded map that you keep on your person or in a secure location, ensuring you can locate your cache even after months or years.

A cache isn't a set-and-forget solution. Periodically checking on your cache ensures it remains intact and undisturbed. Seasonal changes, animal activity, and even natural decay can affect the integrity of your stored supplies. Plan visits during different seasons to assess any potential risks and make necessary adjustments.

During these checks, inspect the containers for signs of damage or moisture intrusion. Refresh the insulating materials if needed and re-camouflage the site if any disturbances are evident. This maintenance helps guarantee that your cache will be reliable when you need it most.

In a survival situation, knowing you have a cache can provide immense peace of mind. When the time comes to retrieve your supplies, approach the location with the same discretion you used to create it. Confirm the landmarks and signs, carefully uncover the cache, and assess the condition of your supplies.

If you need to relocate the cache due to changes in the environment or discovery risk, ensure you prepare a new site with the same meticulous care. Transfer the supplies quickly but cautiously, maintaining their protection and secrecy.

Creating a cache is more than just a practical step in survival; it's a strategy that embodies foresight, resourcefulness, and respect for the natural world. By thoughtfully selecting a location, meticulously preparing and packaging your supplies, and maintaining the cache over time, you build a robust safety net that can sustain you through uncertain times.

This skill, while rooted in necessity, also deepens your connection to the environment and sharpens your survival instincts. Each cache you create becomes a testament to your ability to adapt and thrive in the wilderness, providing not just sustenance but a tangible link to your preparedness and resilience. Through this practice, you gain the confidence to face whatever challenges the wild may present, knowing you have the resources and knowledge to endure.

BOOK 6: NAVIGATION AND TRAVEL

1. MAP READING AND COMPASS USE

1.1 UNDERSTANDING TOPOGRAPHIC MAPS

The most distinctive feature of a topographic map is its contour lines. These lines connect points of equal elevation, creating a three-dimensional perspective of the landscape on a two-dimensional surface. The first step in understanding a topographic map is to grasp how these lines depict the shape and elevation of the terrain.

Each contour line represents a specific elevation level. When these lines are close together, they indicate a steep slope. Conversely, when the lines are spaced further apart, they signify a gentler incline. As you trace your finger along the lines, you can visualize the rise and fall of the land, predicting the challenges and pathways that lie ahead.

Consider a moment when you are planning a hike to a distant ridge. The contour lines reveal not just the route but also the effort required. A series of tightly packed lines suggests a steep climb, demanding strength and endurance. As you plan your path, you might opt for a route where the lines are more spaced, offering a gentler ascent and a more leisurely pace.

Topographic maps are rich with information beyond just elevation. They include a variety of symbols and colors that represent natural and man-made features. Understanding these symbols is key to fully utilizing the map's potential.

Water bodies, such as lakes, rivers, and streams, are typically shown in blue. Forested areas are marked in green, providing a clear indication of where you might find shelter or resources. Trails, roads, and boundaries are depicted with lines of various styles and colors, guiding your journey through both wilderness and developed areas.

Picture yourself following a trail along a river, the blue line on the map paralleling your route. You come across a fork where the river splits, and the map shows a tributary veering off to the right. This feature helps confirm your position and ensures that you remain on course. The map becomes a companion, offering reassurance and direction with each step.

Understanding elevation changes is critical for planning your journey. Topographic maps provide this information through contour intervals, which is the vertical distance between adjacent contour lines. By reading the contour interval, often found in the map legend, you can estimate the total elevation gain or loss along your route.

For instance, if the contour interval is 20 feet and you count ten contour lines between your current position and your destination, you know there is a 200-foot elevation change. This knowledge allows you to prepare for the physical demands of your hike, ensuring you have the necessary energy and resources.

Imagine you're aiming to summit a nearby peak. The contour lines show a series of ridges and plateaus leading to the top. By counting the lines and understanding the intervals, you can gauge the ascent's steepness and plan rest points. The map transforms into a strategic tool, guiding your decisions and enhancing your preparedness.

Topographic maps also help you identify specific landforms, such as hills, valleys, and ridges. Recognizing these features can be vital for navigation and survival. For example, a series of concentric contour lines with higher elevations in the center indicates a hill or mountain. In contrast, a similar pattern with lower elevations in the center represents a depression or valley.

Visualize yourself navigating through a dense forest, the trees obscuring your view of the broader landscape. Your map shows a long, continuous ridge running north to south. By orienting yourself with a compass and following the ridge, you maintain your bearing even when visibility is limited. The ridge becomes a natural guide, leading you through the forest and towards your destination.

Every topographic map includes a legend, a key that explains the symbols and scales used. Familiarizing yourself with the legend is essential for decoding the map's details. The legend typically includes information on contour intervals, symbols for different types of vegetation, water features, and human-made structures.

Consider a scenario where you're seeking a campsite near a reliable water source. The map legend helps you identify symbols for springs, wells, and streams. By cross-referencing these symbols with your current location, you can plan your route to ensure access to fresh water, a critical factor for your comfort and survival.

To truly master topographic maps, practice is essential. Begin by exploring familiar areas with your map, noting how the features depicted correspond to the actual landscape. This hands-on experience helps solidify your understanding and builds confidence in your navigational skills.

Envision a series of training hikes where you deliberately navigate using only your map and compass. Start with well-marked trails and gradually progress to more challenging terrain. Each outing enhances your ability to read the map, interpret the symbols, and make informed decisions based on the terrain.

As you become proficient, you'll find that the topographic map becomes an extension of your senses. It offers a detailed view of the land, guiding you through both the familiar and the unknown. The ability to read and understand these maps transforms your outdoor adventures, providing a foundation of knowledge and confidence that ensures you can explore safely and effectively.

1.2 COMPASS BASICS AND NAVIGATION TECHNIQUES

At its core, a compass consists of a magnetic needle that aligns with the Earth's magnetic field, pointing towards magnetic north. This needle sits within a housing marked with degrees from 0 to 360, representing a full circle. A typical compass also features a rotating bezel, or azimuth ring, with degree markings, and an orienting arrow or lines for precise navigation.

The first step in using a compass is to familiarize yourself with its parts and how they interact. Hold the compass flat in your hand, ensuring the needle can move freely. Rotate yourself until the needle aligns with the orienting arrow. The bezel's degree markings now correspond to the direction you're facing.

Taking a Bearing

Taking a bearing is a fundamental compass skill that involves identifying the direction from your current location to a specific landmark or destination. To do this, hold the compass flat and point the direction of travel arrow at the landmark. Rotate the bezel until the orienting arrow aligns with the magnetic needle. The degree reading at the bezel's index line indicates the bearing to your destination.

Picture yourself standing at the edge of a vast meadow, aiming to reach a distant hill. You lift your compass, sight along the direction of travel arrow, and turn the bezel until the needle is aligned. The bearing reads 75 degrees. With this information, you can confidently navigate towards the hill, adjusting your course as needed to maintain the bearing.

Following a Bearing

Once you have your bearing, the next step is to follow it accurately. This involves moving in the direction indicated by the bearing, using the compass to ensure you stay on course. As you walk, periodically check the compass to verify that the needle remains aligned with the orienting arrow. Adjust your path to correct any deviations. In the dense forest, where visibility is limited, maintaining a straight line can be challenging. Use intermediate landmarks, such as distinctive trees or rocks, to help guide you. Walk to each landmark, then take a new sighting to the next. This technique, known as leapfrogging, helps ensure you stay on course even when the terrain is complex.

Orienting the Map

Integrating your compass skills with a topographic map enhances your navigational accuracy. Orienting the map involves aligning it with the terrain, ensuring that north on the map corresponds with magnetic north. To do this, place the compass on the map with the edge aligned along the north-south grid lines. Rotate the map and compass together until the magnetic needle aligns with the orienting arrow. The map is now oriented to the landscape. Imagine you're navigating through a series of ridges and valleys. By orienting the map, you can accurately identify your position relative to the surrounding features. This alignment allows you to transfer bearings from the map to the compass and vice versa, creating a cohesive navigation strategy.

Triangulation

Triangulation is a technique used to pinpoint your exact location on a map by taking bearings to two or more known landmarks. Start by taking a bearing to the first landmark and drawing a line along that bearing on the map. Repeat this process with a second landmark. The point where the lines intersect is your location.

Envision yourself standing on a ridge with two prominent peaks visible. You take a bearing to each peak and mark these bearings on your map. The intersection of the lines reveals your position, allowing you to navigate with greater confidence.

Magnetic Declination

Magnetic declination is the difference between magnetic north and true north. This variation changes based on your geographic location and can affect compass accuracy if not accounted for. Many compasses allow you to adjust for declination by setting the bezel to the local declination value, ensuring your bearings are accurate.

Consider a scenario where you're hiking in an area with a 10-degree west declination. By adjusting your compass to account for this, you ensure that your bearings align with true north, improving the accuracy of your navigation.

Navigating in Poor Visibility

Navigating in poor visibility, whether due to fog, dense forest, or night conditions, requires heightened reliance on your compass. Use the leapfrogging technique more frequently, selecting close, identifiable landmarks. Take frequent compass readings to stay on course and move cautiously, ensuring you maintain your direction.

Imagine a dense fog rolling in as you cross a meadow. Visibility drops to a few yards, obscuring distant landmarks. Your compass becomes your guide, leading you from one recognizable feature to the next, helping you traverse the challenging conditions without losing your way.

Compass Maintenance and Care

A compass is a delicate instrument that requires proper care to function correctly. Keep it away from magnetic fields, which can alter the needle's alignment. Regularly check the compass for accuracy and ensure it's free from damage. Store it in a protective case to prevent scratches and breakage.

Maintaining your compass ensures it remains a reliable tool, ready to guide you through any adventure. Treat it with the respect it deserves, knowing that in critical moments, its accuracy and reliability are paramount.

1.3 NAVIGATING WITHOUT A COMPASS

In the vast wilderness, there may come a time when you find yourself without a compass. Whether it's lost, broken, or simply left behind, the ability to navigate without this essential tool is a critical skill for any outdoor adventurer. Learning to rely on natural indicators and your instincts can guide you safely through the most challenging environments.

Using the Sun and Shadows

The sun is one of the most reliable natural indicators for navigation. In the northern hemisphere, the sun rises in the east and sets in the west. Around midday, it is typically in the southern part of the sky. Observing the sun's position can help you determine cardinal directions.

To use the sun for navigation, start by finding an open area where you can see the horizon. In the morning, stand with your right arm pointing towards where the sun rises. Your left arm will point west, your face north, and your back south. This simple alignment gives you a rough sense of direction.

A more precise method involves using a shadow stick. Place a straight stick vertically into the ground and mark the tip of its shadow with a small stone. Wait about 15-20 minutes, then mark the new position of the shadow tip. Draw a line between the two marks to create an east-west line. Standing with the first mark (west) to your left and the second mark (east) to your right, you will be facing north.

Navigating by the Stars

When the sun is no longer visible, the night sky becomes your guide. The North Star, or Polaris, is a constant beacon for navigators in the northern hemisphere. It is found by locating the Big Dipper, a prominent constellation. The two stars at the end of the Big Dipper's bowl point directly to Polaris, which is part of the Little Dipper constellation. Once you have located Polaris, you can determine true north.

Imagine standing in an open field, the stars shining brightly above. By finding the North Star, you can maintain a sense of direction throughout the night. Remember that while Polaris is a fixed point, the other stars move in a circular pattern around it, offering additional cues for direction.

Observing Natural Landmarks

Nature is full of landmarks that can aid in navigation. Mountains, rivers, and valleys often run in specific directions that can help orient you. For instance, rivers generally flow downhill and can lead you to lower elevations and potentially to civilization.

Consider a dense forest with a distant mountain range. By identifying a prominent peak or a unique rock formation, you can use it as a reference point. This helps maintain your direction even when the terrain becomes confusing. In open areas, look for distinctive trees, large boulders, or other natural features that stand out and can be used as waypoints.

Using Vegetation and Environmental Clues

Plants and trees can provide subtle hints about direction. In the northern hemisphere, moss typically grows thicker on the north side of trees where it is more shaded. However, this is not a foolproof method, as moss growth can be influenced by local conditions.

Trees can also offer clues. For example, the branches of trees on the southern side often grow more densely due to greater exposure to sunlight. Observing the general growth patterns of vegetation can help you infer cardinal directions.

Following Water Sources

Water sources like streams and rivers are natural guides. In many regions, rivers eventually lead to larger bodies of water, which may be near towns or roads. Following a river downstream can be a practical way to find your way out of the wilderness. Imagine you've come across a flowing stream. By tracing its course, you not only maintain a consistent direction but also ensure access to fresh water. This strategy can be especially useful in mountainous areas where streams flow from higher elevations to valleys below.

Tracking Animal Behavior

Animals are attuned to their environment and can inadvertently provide navigation clues. For instance, game trails often lead to water sources or open areas.

Birds, especially in the morning and evening, tend to fly towards water bodies. Following these natural indicators can help you navigate more effectively. Picture yourself observing a herd of deer moving purposefully through the forest. By following their trail, you may be led to water sources or natural clearings that offer better visibility and orientation.

Constructing Makeshift Compasses

In an emergency, you can create a simple compass using a magnetized needle, a leaf, and a small pool of water. Magnetize the needle by stroking it with silk or rubbing it on a magnet, then carefully place it on the leaf floating on water. The needle will align itself north-south, providing a basic directional guide.

2. TERRAIN ANALYSIS

2.1 GAUGING TERRAIN AND OBSTACLES

In the wilderness, understanding the terrain and recognizing potential obstacles is crucial for safe and efficient navigation. Gauging the landscape accurately allows you to plan routes, avoid hazards, and make informed decisions that can significantly impact your journey. This section delves into the techniques and insights necessary for analyzing terrain and identifying obstacles, equipping you with the skills to navigate even the most challenging environments.

Visualizing the Terrain

The first step in gauging terrain is to develop an eye for the natural features around you. This involves not only looking at what is immediately visible but also imagining the unseen elements. Hills, valleys, ridges, and plains each tell a story about the land's formation and the paths that lie ahead.

As you scan the horizon, notice the way the ground rises and falls. Hills and mountains are obvious high points, but also look for subtler inclines and declines. Valleys, often formed by rivers or streams, can guide you towards water sources or serve as natural pathways through the landscape. Ridges provide elevated routes that can offer better visibility and easier travel in some terrains.

Consider the interplay of light and shadow as the sun moves across the sky. Shadows cast by hills and ridges can help you gauge the height and steepness of these features. For example, long, stretched shadows indicate gentle slopes, while short, sharp shadows suggest steep inclines.

Using Landmarks and Natural Features

Landmarks are essential for orientation and navigation. They help you maintain your bearings and can serve as checkpoints along your route. Look for prominent natural features such as solitary trees, unique rock formations, or distinct peaks. These landmarks not only help you navigate but also offer reference points to gauge distance and direction.

Imagine trekking through a dense forest. Your visibility is limited, but ahead, you spot a towering rock outcrop. This outcrop becomes a guiding beacon, helping you maintain a straight course through the trees. By consistently orienting yourself towards this landmark, you avoid the common pitfall of veering off course in dense terrain.

Assessing Obstacles

Obstacles in the wilderness come in many forms, from physical barriers like rivers and cliffs to less obvious challenges such as dense underbrush or unstable ground. Identifying and assessing these obstacles early allows you to plan alternative routes or prepare for the challenges they present.

Rivers and streams, while valuable for their water, can be significant obstacles. Assess their width, depth, and flow rate before attempting to cross. In some cases, it might be safer to follow the waterway until you find a natural bridge or a safer crossing point.

Cliffs and steep inclines require careful consideration. Attempting to climb or descend without proper gear and experience can be dangerous. Instead, look for gentler slopes or natural pathways that provide a safer route.

Dense vegetation, such as thick underbrush or tangled vines, can slow your progress and obscure potential hazards. When faced with such terrain, consider skirting around it or finding a game trail that might offer a clearer path.

Utilizing Elevation and Contours

Understanding elevation changes is crucial for efficient travel. Ascending and descending steep slopes can be physically demanding and time-consuming. By recognizing these changes in advance, you can choose routes that minimize unnecessary climbs and descents.

Use your knowledge of contour lines from topographic maps to interpret the terrain. Contour lines that are close together indicate steep slopes, while those spaced further apart suggest gentler terrain. By aligning your path with the natural contours of the land, you can conserve energy and travel more efficiently.

Adapting to Different Environments

Different environments present unique challenges and opportunities. Each type of terrain—whether it's a forest, desert, mountainous region, or wetland—requires specific strategies for navigation.

In forests, the dense canopy can limit visibility and obscure landmarks. Here, undergrowth can impede progress, and fallen logs or thick brush can create physical barriers. Use natural clearings and trails to your advantage, and keep an eye out for animal paths that often lead to water sources or easier terrain.

Deserts, with their vast, open spaces and minimal landmarks, pose a different set of challenges. Navigation relies heavily on distant features such as dunes or rock formations. The sun's position can guide you, but be aware of the risk of dehydration and the difficulty of travel in loose sand.

Mountains demand respect for their sheer physicality. The combination of elevation, weather, and rugged terrain requires careful planning. Use ridges and valleys to your advantage, understanding that high altitudes can affect your endurance and breathing. Be prepared for sudden weather changes and the possibility of encountering snow or ice.

Wetlands and marshes can be treacherous, with hidden water channels and unstable ground. Look for solid ground and natural levees to traverse these areas safely. Avoid deep mud and quicksand, which can pose significant dangers.

2.2 STRATEGIC ROUTE PLANNING

The first step in route planning is to clearly define your objective. Whether you're aiming to summit a distant peak, reach a secluded campsite, or traverse a remote valley, your goal shapes every aspect of your plan. Consider the distance, elevation changes, and the nature of the terrain. This understanding allows you to anticipate challenges and allocate time and resources effectively.

For instance, a trek to a high-altitude lake requires different preparations than a journey through dense forest. Each objective demands its own set of considerations, from the gear you carry to the pace you set.

Studying the Terrain

With your objective in mind, turn your attention to the map. Examine the terrain in detail, noting the contours, landmarks, and potential obstacles. Hills, valleys, ridges, and water bodies all influence your route. The contour lines reveal elevation changes, helping you gauge the difficulty of different sections.

Visualize yourself moving through this landscape. Imagine the steep climbs, the gentle descents, the rivers you'll cross, and the ridges you'll follow. This mental rehearsal prepares you for the physical demands of the journey and helps you identify the best routes.

Consider a hike through a mountainous region. The map shows a series of ridges running parallel to each other. By planning a route that follows these ridges, you minimize unnecessary elevation changes and enjoy panoramic views that guide your way.

Prioritizing Safety and Efficiency

Safety is paramount in route planning. Choose routes that avoid hazardous areas like steep cliffs, unstable slopes, and dense underbrush. Look for natural pathways, such as valleys and ridges, that offer easier travel and better visibility.

Efficiency is also crucial. A direct route is often preferable, but not if it leads through difficult terrain. Sometimes, a longer but gentler path saves time and energy in the long run. For example, a circuitous route around a swamp is safer and quicker than attempting to slog through it.

As you plan, think about the resources you'll need. Ensure your route provides access to water sources, and plan for rest stops at regular intervals. These considerations prevent exhaustion and dehydration, keeping you strong and alert throughout the journey.

Flexibility and Contingency Planning

No matter how detailed your plan, the wilderness is unpredictable. Weather changes, unexpected obstacles, and physical fatigue can all alter your course. Building flexibility into your plan allows you to adapt to these variables without jeopardizing your safety.

Identify potential alternate routes and escape paths. These contingencies provide options if your primary route becomes impassable. For example, if a river crossing proves too dangerous, a nearby bridge or a shallower section upstream might offer a safer alternative.

Imagine trekking through a forest when a sudden storm hits. Your planned route crosses an exposed ridge that is now unsafe. A quick glance at your map shows a lower, forested path that offers shelter from the wind and rain. This flexibility ensures you can continue your journey safely, even when conditions change.

Timing and Pacing

Effective route planning involves careful timing and pacing. Estimate how long each segment of your journey will take, considering the terrain, weather, and your physical condition. Plan for slower progress through difficult areas and faster travel on easy ground.

Pacing yourself is essential to avoid exhaustion. Start at a steady, moderate pace, allowing your body to warm up and adjust to the physical demands. As you progress, take regular breaks to rest and refuel. This rhythm maintains your energy levels and reduces the risk of injury.

Consider a multi-day trek with a high-altitude summit. Your first day might involve a gradual ascent to a base camp, followed by a rest day to acclimatize. The final push to the summit is planned for early morning, taking advantage of stable weather and allowing plenty of time for a safe descent.

Navigational Aids and Technology

While traditional map and compass skills are invaluable, modern technology can enhance your route planning. GPS devices and smartphone apps provide real-time location tracking, helping you stay on course. However, technology should complement, not replace, your fundamental navigational skills.

Use these tools to cross-reference your position, track your progress, and make adjustments as needed. Always carry extra batteries or a solar charger to ensure your devices remain operational. And remember, technology can fail—so your map, compass, and the skills to use them are your primary navigational tools.

Environmental and Ethical Considerations

Respecting the environment is a crucial aspect of route planning. Choose paths that minimize your impact on the land, avoiding fragile ecosystems and staying on established trails where possible. This practice preserves the wilderness for future adventurers and protects the habitats of wildlife.

Ethical considerations also include preparedness and self-reliance. Plan your route with the expectation of encountering no outside assistance. Carry sufficient supplies, know your limits, and inform someone of your itinerary and expected return. This preparation ensures you are a responsible and respectful visitor to the wilderness.

2.3 WEATHER AND ENVIRONMENTAL FACTORS

Understanding weather and environmental factors is crucial for any outdoor expedition. These elements can significantly impact your journey, influencing not only your comfort and safety but also the terrain itself. By recognizing and adapting to these factors, you can enhance your preparedness and resilience, ensuring a more successful and enjoyable adventure.

Reading the Sky

The sky is a vast and dynamic indicator of weather patterns. Learning to interpret its signs can provide valuable foresight into impending conditions. Clear skies with a deep blue hue suggest stable weather, ideal for long hikes and open trails. However, a sky filled with towering, white cumulus clouds can indicate fair weather but also the potential for afternoon thunderstorms, particularly in mountainous regions.

As you hike, keep an eye on the horizon. Dark, anvil-shaped cumulonimbus clouds signal severe weather, often bringing heavy rain, thunder, and lightning. The sight of these clouds forming should prompt you to seek shelter and reevaluate your route. Storms in the wilderness can be sudden and intense, transforming benign terrain into a hazardous landscape.

Consider a day in the high mountains. The morning starts clear, but by midday, you notice dark clouds gathering in the west. Recognizing the signs, you decide to descend to a lower elevation, where you can find shelter and avoid the brunt of the storm. This decision, informed by your awareness of the sky, keeps you safe and dry.

Wind and Its Implications

Wind patterns offer another layer of insight into weather conditions. A gentle breeze can be refreshing, but sudden gusts or shifts in wind direction often precede changes in the weather. Strong, sustained winds can indicate an approaching front, bringing cooler temperatures and precipitation.

Pay attention to the wind's effect on the environment. In forests, swaying trees and rustling leaves are immediate indicators. On open terrain, dust devils or the movement of grasses and shrubs reveal wind patterns. In the desert, the wind can shape the dunes, providing clues about prevailing directions.

Imagine traversing a coastal area where the wind picks up suddenly, bringing with it the scent of the sea and a drop in temperature. You understand that a cold front is moving in, prompting you to find a sheltered spot to set up camp. Your ability to read the wind ensures you're prepared for the change.

Temperature Variations

Temperature plays a critical role in your journey, affecting not only your comfort but also the terrain. Rapid changes in temperature, especially in mountainous areas, can be challenging. Mornings might be chilly, with frost covering the ground, while afternoons warm up considerably. This fluctuation requires layering your clothing to manage body heat effectively.

In higher altitudes, temperatures can drop sharply as the sun sets. Hypothermia becomes a risk if you're not prepared with appropriate gear. Conversely, in desert environments, daytime heat can be extreme, and the drop in temperature at night can be just as severe.

Think about a trek through a canyon in the desert southwest. As the sun climbs, the temperature rises dramatically. You pace yourself, hydrate regularly, and seek shade during the hottest parts of the day. As evening approaches, you add layers to protect against the cold. This strategic management of temperature ensures your safety and endurance.

Precipitation and Its Effects

Rain, snow, and ice transform the landscape, creating new challenges and hazards. Rain can swell rivers and streams, making crossings dangerous. It can also turn trails into slippery, muddy obstacles. Snow and ice add another layer of difficulty, obscuring paths and increasing the risk of hypothermia and frostbite.

Before setting out, check the weather forecast and understand the typical precipitation patterns for the region. Equip yourself with waterproof gear, including a sturdy tent, rain jacket, and dry bags to protect your supplies. If snow is a possibility, carry traction devices like crampons and an ice axe for safe travel.

Envision a scenario where you're hiking along a well-trodden trail when a sudden downpour begins. The path quickly becomes slick and treacherous. By having waterproof gear and a solid understanding of the terrain, you find an elevated spot to wait out the worst of the rain, then continue cautiously once it subsides.

Seasonal Considerations

Different seasons bring distinct challenges and opportunities. Spring might offer blooming flowers and flowing rivers, but also unpredictable weather and swollen streams from snowmelt. Summer provides long days and warm temperatures, but the risk of thunderstorms and extreme heat. Autumn's cooler temperatures and vibrant foliage are balanced by shorter days and the onset of early snows. Winter transforms the landscape with snow and ice, demanding specialized gear and skills. Plan your trips with these seasonal variations in mind. Recognize that a route easy to navigate in summer could be impassable in winter. Adjust your plans and gear accordingly, ensuring you're prepared for the specific conditions of each season.

Picture a late autumn hike in a deciduous forest. The crisp air and colorful leaves create a picturesque scene, but you're mindful of the shorter daylight hours and the potential for early snow. You set a steady pace, plan your route to maximize daylight, and carry extra layers to guard against the cold.

Wildlife and Environmental Interactions

Weather and environmental factors also influence wildlife behavior, which can impact your journey. Animals seek shelter during storms, come out to forage during clear weather, and migrate with the seasons. Understanding these patterns helps you anticipate encounters and navigate the terrain safely.

In bear country, for example, knowing that bears are more active at dawn and dusk can guide your campsite choices and food storage practices. In areas with venomous snakes, being aware that they bask in the sun can help you avoid their habitats during peak activity times.

Imagine hiking through a region known for its wildlife. You're aware that the changing seasons bring different animals into the area. By understanding their behavior, you choose campsites away from their trails and stay vigilant, reducing the risk of unwanted encounters.

Adaptation and Preparedness

Adapting to weather and environmental factors requires a blend of preparation and flexibility. Always carry essential gear for a range of conditions, and be ready to adjust your plans based on real-time observations. This readiness not only enhances your safety but also allows you to fully appreciate the dynamic beauty of the wilderness.

3. Long-Distance Travel Techniques

3.1 Energy Conservation Strategies

One of the most fundamental aspects of energy conservation is finding and maintaining a steady pace. It's tempting to start a journey with a burst of energy, but this can lead to quick exhaustion. Instead, aim for a pace that feels sustainable over long distances. This often means starting slower than you might expect, allowing your body to warm up and adjust to the physical demands.

Think of your journey as a marathon, not a sprint. By establishing a consistent rhythm, you can travel longer without tiring quickly. Listen to your body's signals, finding a cadence that balances speed with endurance. Each step should feel deliberate and controlled, conserving energy with every movement.

Rest and Recovery

Regular rest breaks are essential for maintaining energy levels. These pauses allow your muscles to recover and prevent fatigue from setting in. Plan for short breaks every hour or so, and longer rests for meals or significant landmarks. During these breaks, take the time to hydrate, eat, and stretch your muscles.

Imagine hiking through a dense forest. After a steady hour of walking, you find a fallen log beside a bubbling brook. This is an ideal spot for a short rest. Sit down, sip some water, eat a snack, and enjoy the sound of the stream. These moments of rest rejuvenate your body and mind, preparing you for the next leg of your journey.

Efficient Packing

The weight of your pack has a direct impact on your energy expenditure. Pack only essential items, and distribute the weight evenly to prevent strain on your back and shoulders. Each item should serve a specific purpose, and multipurpose tools are invaluable.

Consider the contents of your pack carefully. Lightweight, high-calorie foods provide the necessary energy without adding bulk. Clothing should be appropriate for the weather, allowing for layering to manage body temperature. A well-organized pack, with frequently used items easily accessible, minimizes the effort required to retrieve them.

Hydration and Nutrition

Proper hydration is critical for energy conservation. Dehydration leads to fatigue and decreased physical performance, so drink water regularly, even if you don't feel thirsty. In hot or dry environments, increase your water intake to compensate for higher fluid loss.

Nutrition is equally important. Consuming balanced meals that include carbohydrates, proteins, and fats provides sustained energy. Snacks like nuts, dried fruits, and energy bars can keep your energy levels stable between meals. Plan your meals to coincide with your longer rest breaks, allowing your body to digest and absorb nutrients effectively.

Imagine a long trek through arid terrain. The sun beats down, and you feel the moisture evaporating from your skin. Regular sips of water from your canteen keep you hydrated. At midday, you stop in the shade of a large rock, eat a balanced meal, and rest. This routine keeps your energy steady and prevents the debilitating effects of dehydration and hunger.

Terrain Management

Navigating different terrains requires adapting your energy expenditure. Uphill climbs are particularly demanding, so take smaller steps and maintain a steady pace to avoid overexertion. Use zigzag patterns on steep inclines to reduce strain. Downhill sections, while less tiring on the cardiovascular system, can be tough on joints and muscles. Use controlled, deliberate steps to prevent injury.

In flat or rolling terrain, focus on maintaining a consistent rhythm. Conserve energy by using efficient walking techniques, such as the rolling step, where you place your heel down first, then roll through to your toes. This method reduces the impact on your feet and legs, conserving energy over long distances.

Picture yourself on a steep mountain trail. The ascent is challenging, but by taking small, measured steps and zigzagging across the path, you conserve energy and maintain a steady pace. As you reach the summit, the descent requires careful, controlled movements to protect your knees and ankles. Each adjustment to your walking technique helps manage your energy reserves effectively.

Mental Focus and Motivation

Maintaining mental focus and motivation is crucial for long-distance travel. Fatigue can be as much a mental challenge as a physical one. Setting small, achievable goals helps break the journey into manageable segments.

Celebrate reaching each milestone, whether it's a specific distance, a landmark, or a scheduled rest break.

Positive self-talk and visualization techniques can bolster your mental resilience. Picture yourself completing the journey, feeling strong and accomplished. Remind yourself of the purpose of your trek and the rewards awaiting you. Mental strength and a positive attitude can carry you through the most challenging parts of your journey.

Imagine the sun setting as you near the end of a long day's hike. The last few miles are the hardest, but you focus on reaching the next visible landmark, a large oak tree at the edge of the trail. With each step, you remind yourself of the sense of achievement waiting at your campsite. This mental focus keeps you moving forward, conserving energy by maintaining a positive and determined mindset.

Weather and Environmental Adaptation

Adapting to weather conditions is another key aspect of energy conservation. In hot weather, travel during the cooler parts of the day—early morning and late afternoon. Use midday for rest and hydration in shaded areas. Wear lightweight, breathable clothing to regulate body temperature. In cold weather, dress in layers to manage body heat efficiently. Stay dry by avoiding sweat buildup, which can lead to hypothermia. Adjust your pace to prevent overheating or excessive sweating. Understanding and adapting to the weather conditions help conserve energy and maintain your health. Picture yourself on a cold, windy day. You start with several layers of clothing, gradually shedding them as your body warms up. Your pace is steady, preventing sweat buildup, and you take breaks in sheltered spots to avoid the wind's chilling effects. These adaptations help you maintain a comfortable body temperature, conserving energy for the journey ahead.

3.2 CROSSING WATER BODIES SAFELY

Before attempting any water crossing, it is crucial to assess the situation thoroughly. The first step is to evaluate the water's depth, speed, and temperature. Fast-moving water can be deceptively strong, capable of sweeping you off your feet even at shallow depths. Cold water presents the risk of hypothermia, which can quickly sap your strength and coordination. Approach the water's edge and use a long stick or trekking pole to gauge the depth. Watch for debris and floating objects, which indicate strong currents. Look downstream for potential hazards such as rocks, fallen trees, or rapids. Identifying these dangers early helps you plan a safer route across.

Imagine a scenario where you're faced with a river swollen from recent rains. The water is murky, and you can see branches and logs being carried downstream. You realize that crossing here could be perilous, and you decide to scout upstream for a safer crossing point where the water might be calmer and shallower.

Finding the best place to cross is essential. Look for wide, shallow sections where the current is slower. These areas are often found where the river or stream widens, reducing the water's velocity. Avoid narrow sections, which tend to have faster currents and deeper water.

Search for natural fords—places where the riverbed is more stable, such as gravel bars or sandy bottoms. Rocky areas can be slippery and uneven, posing additional risks. If the water is too deep or the current too strong, consider finding an alternative route, such as a fallen log or a natural bridge.

Picture yourself scouting along a riverbank. You find a spot where the water spreads out over a wide gravel bar, the current gentle and clear. The riverbed here is visible and appears stable. This is an ideal crossing point, offering both safety and ease of passage.

Preparation is key to a successful water crossing. Secure all loose items in your pack and use waterproof bags to protect your gear. Remove any clothing that could become heavy when wet, such as jackets and boots, and consider crossing in lightweight, quick-drying clothes.

Use a sturdy stick or trekking pole for balance. This third point of contact helps you maintain stability against the current. If traveling in a group, link arms or hold onto a rope for added support. This creates a human chain that provides mutual assistance and stability.

Imagine preparing to cross a stream with a swift current. You secure your backpack with waterproof covers, remove your boots, and put on lightweight sandals. Using your trekking pole for balance, you and your companions link arms, forming a line to support each other against the force of the water. When crossing, face upstream and move sideways, maintaining a stable stance. This allows you to lean into the current and reduce its impact on your balance. Take small, deliberate steps, feeling for secure footing with each move. Avoid lifting your feet too high, which can cause you to lose balance.

Use the pole or stick to probe the riverbed ahead of you, ensuring solid ground. If the water is deep, consider using a modified breaststroke, pushing the pole or stick against the bottom for propulsion and stability.

In situations where the current is exceptionally strong, crossing as a group can provide additional safety. Form a line with the strongest member upstream to break the current, and the others following close behind. This technique minimizes individual exposure to the full force of the water.

Picture yourself crossing a wide, shallow river. The water reaches your knees, and the current tugs at your legs. By facing upstream and moving sideways, you lean into the flow, using your pole to steady each step. Your companions follow in your footsteps, the linked line providing mutual support and confidence.

For deeper crossings, where wading is not feasible, consider swimming. However, this should only be attempted by strong swimmers and when the water is warm enough to prevent hypothermia. Keep your pack on your back if it floats or use it as a flotation aid if it's waterproof.

Swim diagonally downstream to conserve energy, letting the current assist your progress. Aim for a point slightly upstream of your intended exit to account for the downstream drift. Be cautious of submerged obstacles and stay calm, conserving energy with controlled strokes.

Imagine a wide, deep river that requires swimming. You secure your pack as a flotation aid and enter the water, swimming at an angle downstream. The current helps carry you across, and you maintain a steady, controlled pace, keeping your exit point in sight.

Once you've crossed, take the time to rest and dry off. Change into dry clothes to prevent hypothermia and check your gear for any water damage. Take a moment to reassess your route and ensure everyone in your group is ready to continue. Drying out not only prevents cold-related issues but also helps avoid blisters and other discomforts that can arise from hiking in wet clothing and footwear.

3.3 DEALING WITH EXTREME CONDITIONS

In the scorching heat, the first rule is to avoid the midday sun. Plan your travel for the early morning and late afternoon when temperatures are cooler. Use the midday hours to rest in the shade, conserving your energy and avoiding heatstroke.

Hydration is critical. Drink water regularly, even if you don't feel thirsty. Dehydration can set in quickly, sapping your strength and clarity of thought. Carry sufficient water and know where to find natural sources along your route. If possible, use a water purification system to ensure safe drinking water.

Imagine trekking through a desert landscape. You set out at dawn, the air still cool. As the sun rises higher, you find a shaded spot under a rocky overhang and rest through the hottest part of the day. In the late afternoon, you resume your journey, the temperatures more bearable. This routine helps you manage the extreme heat effectively.

Wearing appropriate clothing is also crucial. Lightweight, loose-fitting clothes provide protection from the sun and allow your body to cool naturally. A wide-brimmed hat shields your face and neck, while sunglasses protect your eyes from the glare. Apply sunscreen to exposed skin to prevent burns.

Coping with Extreme Cold

Now imagine a different scenario: you are traversing a snowy wilderness, the cold biting into your skin. The landscape is a pristine white, beautiful yet deadly. Dealing with extreme cold requires layering your clothing to maintain body heat without causing excessive sweating, which can lead to hypothermia.

Start with a moisture-wicking base layer to keep sweat away from your skin. Add insulating layers, such as fleece or down, to trap body heat. The outer layer should be windproof and waterproof, protecting you from the elements. Adjust your layers as needed to avoid overheating or getting too cold.

Keep your extremities warm with insulated gloves, a hat, and sturdy boots. The head and hands lose heat rapidly, so covering them is essential. In extreme cold, take regular breaks to check for signs of frostbite and hypothermia among your group. Picture a trek through a snow-covered forest. The air is frigid, but you are well-prepared with layered clothing. You adjust your layers as you move, ensuring you stay warm without sweating. At each rest stop, you check your fingers and toes for numbness, staying vigilant against the cold.

Navigating through Storms

Storms, whether they bring rain, snow, or wind, pose a significant challenge. Navigating through a storm requires finding shelter and waiting out the worst of the weather if possible. Lightning, strong winds, and heavy precipitation can create dangerous conditions that make travel nearly impossible.

Seek natural shelters, such as caves, overhangs, or dense forests, to protect yourself from the elements. If no natural shelter is available, use a tarp or tent to create a makeshift shelter. Ensure it is secure and can withstand strong winds.

Imagine being caught in a sudden mountain storm. Dark clouds gather quickly, and the wind picks up. You find a rocky overhang and use your tarp to create a windbreak. As the storm rages, you stay dry and sheltered, waiting for the weather to pass before continuing your journey.

Stay dry during storms to prevent hypothermia. Wet clothes lose their insulating properties, making it harder to stay warm. Waterproof gear, including jackets, pants, and covers for your pack, is essential. Avoid crossing rivers or streams during heavy rain, as they can swell rapidly and become dangerous.

Adapting to High Altitudes

High altitudes bring their own set of challenges, including thinner air, colder temperatures, and increased UV radiation. Acclimatization is key to avoiding altitude sickness, which can range from mild headaches to severe, life-threatening conditions. Ascend gradually, allowing your body time to adjust to the reduced oxygen levels. Stay hydrated and avoid alcohol and tobacco, which can exacerbate symptoms. If you experience severe symptoms of altitude sickness, such as shortness of breath, confusion, or loss of coordination, descend immediately.

Consider a climb to a high mountain pass. You take your time, ascending slowly and taking regular breaks. You drink plenty of water and monitor your body's response to the altitude. This careful approach ensures you adapt to the thin air without overexerting yourself.

Mental Resilience and Preparation

Dealing with extreme conditions also demands mental resilience. The psychological stress of enduring harsh environments can be as challenging as the physical demands.

Maintaining a positive mindset, staying focused on your goals, and having confidence in your skills are crucial. Prepare mentally by visualizing potential challenges and your responses. This mental rehearsal helps you stay calm and make rational decisions when faced with real difficulties. Having a clear plan and knowing that you are equipped to handle the conditions boosts your confidence and determination. Imagine preparing for a long-distance trek through varied and extreme environments. You visualize the heat of the desert, the cold of the mountains, and the ferocity of storms. You see yourself navigating these challenges with confidence and resilience, prepared for whatever comes your way. This mental preparation is as important as your physical readiness.

BOOK 7: HEALTH AND FIRST AID

1. BASIC FIRST AID

1.1 TREATING CUTS, BURNS, AND BITES

Treating injuries in the wilderness is a critical skill for any adventurer. Cuts, burns, and bites are common occurrences that can escalate quickly if not properly managed. Understanding how to address these injuries with basic first aid ensures that you can maintain health and safety in remote locations, far from immediate medical help.

Cuts can vary from minor scrapes to deep lacerations. The first step in treating any cut is to stop the bleeding. Apply direct pressure to the wound using a clean cloth or bandage. Elevate the injured area above the heart level to reduce blood flow and assist in clotting.

Once the bleeding is controlled, clean the wound thoroughly. Use clean water to rinse out dirt and debris. If available, an antiseptic solution can help prevent infection. Gently pat the area dry with a sterile cloth or gauze.

Imagine your leg is bleeding profusely from a deep cut. You quickly press a bandana against the wound, applying firm pressure. After a few minutes, the bleeding slows, and you find a nearby stream to wash out the dirt. You then use a small bottle of antiseptic from your first aid kit to disinfect the wound before dressing it.

After cleaning the wound, apply an antibiotic ointment to reduce the risk of infection. Cover the cut with a sterile bandage, ensuring it is secure but not too tight. Check the wound regularly for signs of infection, such as increased redness, swelling, or pus. If you notice any of these symptoms, it may be necessary to seek medical attention.

Burns can occur from various sources, including campfires, hot surfaces, or even prolonged sun exposure. The severity of burns ranges from minor first-degree burns to more serious third-degree burns.

For minor burns, the first step is to cool the affected area. Run cool (not cold) water over the burn for at least 10 to 20 minutes. This helps to reduce pain and swelling. Avoid using ice, as it can cause further tissue damage.

Imagine you accidentally touch a hot cooking pot, resulting in a painful burn on your hand. You immediately immerse your hand in a nearby stream, allowing the cool water to soothe the burn. The pain gradually subsides, and you proceed to the next steps of treatment.

After cooling the burn, gently pat the area dry with a clean cloth. Apply an over-the-counter burn ointment or aloe vera gel to soothe the skin and prevent infection. Cover the burn with a sterile, non-stick bandage to protect it from further injury.

For more severe burns, where the skin is blistered or charred, it is crucial to seek medical help as soon as possible. Do not attempt to break blisters or remove charred clothing stuck to the skin. Instead, cover the burn with a clean cloth and keep the injured person hydrated until help arrives.

Bites from insects, snakes, and other animals can pose serious health risks, including allergic reactions, infections, and venomous effects. Prompt and appropriate treatment is essential.

For insect bites and stings, start by removing any stingers left in the skin. Use a credit card or similar object to scrape it out gently. Avoid using tweezers, as squeezing the stinger can release more venom. Wash the area with soap and water, then apply an antiseptic.

Imagine you're stung by a bee. You feel a sharp pain and notice the stinger still in your skin. Using a plastic card from your wallet, you scrape out the stinger, then wash the area thoroughly with water and soap. You apply a dab of antiseptic cream and take an antihistamine to reduce swelling and itching.

For snake bites, it is crucial to stay calm and keep the affected limb immobilized at or below heart level. Do not attempt to suck out the venom or use a tourniquet. Clean the bite area with soap and water, and cover it with a clean, dry dressing. Seek emergency medical help immediately, as antivenom treatment may be necessary. Imagine being bitten by a snake while hiking. You feel a sudden, sharp pain and see two puncture marks on your ankle. Keeping your movements minimal, you clean the bite area and wrap it with a sterile bandage. You signal for help, knowing that time is of the essence in getting medical treatment.

For animal bites, such as those from dogs or wild animals, the risk of infection is high. Clean the wound thoroughly with soap and water, and apply an antiseptic. Cover the bite with a sterile bandage and monitor for signs of infection. Rabies is a concern with some animal bites, so seek medical attention to determine if rabies prophylaxis is necessary.

In any first aid situation, there are some general principles to keep in mind. First, always wash your hands or use gloves before treating a wound to prevent infection. Second, stay calm and reassure the injured person, as panic can exacerbate the situation. Third, if you're unsure about the severity of an injury, it's better to seek professional medical advice.

Imagine you're part of a group hiking in a remote area, and one member gets injured. You take a moment to wash your hands with water from your bottle, put on a pair of gloves from your first aid kit, and calmly assess the situation. Your calm demeanor helps reassure the injured person, making the situation more manageable.

1.2 MANAGING ILLNESS IN THE WILDERNESS

Illness can strike unexpectedly in the wilderness, far from the comforts and resources of civilization. Managing illness in such an environment requires a blend of preparedness, knowledge, and calm decision-making. Whether dealing with gastrointestinal issues, respiratory infections, or dehydration, understanding how to recognize and treat these conditions can make all the difference in ensuring a safe and successful outdoor adventure.

Gastrointestinal Issues

Gastrointestinal problems are among the most common ailments in the wilderness, often caused by contaminated food or water. Symptoms can include nausea, vomiting, diarrhea, and abdominal pain. These issues not only make you feel miserable but can also lead to dehydration, which is a serious concern.

The first step in managing gastrointestinal issues is to prevent them. Always treat water from natural sources by boiling, filtering, or using chemical purifiers. Practice good hygiene, such as washing hands before eating and after using the bathroom. When preparing food, ensure that it is cooked thoroughly and stored properly.

Imagine you're on a multi-day hike and suddenly develop diarrhea. The immediate concern is dehydration. Increase your fluid intake, sipping small amounts of water frequently. If you have oral rehydration salts, mix them with water to restore lost electrolytes. Avoid eating solid foods until your symptoms subside, then start with bland items like rice or crackers.

Respiratory Infections

Respiratory infections can range from the common cold to more severe conditions like bronchitis or pneumonia. Symptoms often include coughing, sore throat, congestion, and fever. In the wilderness, these symptoms can be exacerbated by exposure to cold, damp environments.

Rest is crucial for managing respiratory infections. Find a sheltered spot to set up camp, where you can stay warm and dry. Drink plenty of fluids to stay hydrated and help thin mucus. Warm liquids, like herbal teas, can be particularly soothing. Over-the-counter medications, such as acetaminophen or ibuprofen, can help reduce fever and alleviate pain.

Picture yourself nestled in a sleeping bag, sipping hot tea while listening to the rain outside your tent. You've taken the time to rest and hydrate, allowing your body to fight off the infection. Gradually, your symptoms begin to ease, and you regain the strength needed to continue your journey.

Dehydration

Dehydration is a serious risk in the wilderness, especially during strenuous activities or in hot weather. Symptoms include dry mouth, dark urine, dizziness, and fatigue. Preventing dehydration is easier than treating it, so make hydration a priority.

Always carry enough water and have a means to purify more. Drink regularly, even if you're not thirsty, and pay attention to your body's signals. If you notice signs of dehydration, stop and rest in a shaded area. Sip water slowly to avoid overwhelming your stomach, and consider adding electrolytes to your water if you have them.

Imagine hiking under a blazing sun, your mouth dry and your energy waning. Recognizing the signs of dehydration, you find a shaded spot and take a break. You slowly drink water, feeling your strength return. By addressing the issue promptly, you prevent a mild problem from becoming a serious threat.

Altitude Sickness

Altitude sickness can occur when you ascend too quickly to high elevations without allowing your body time to acclimate. Symptoms include headache, nausea, dizziness, and shortness of breath. In severe cases, it can lead to life-threatening conditions like high-altitude pulmonary edema (HAPE) or high-altitude cerebral edema (HACE).

The best way to manage altitude sickness is to prevent it through gradual acclimatization. Ascend slowly, allowing time for your body to adjust. Stay well-hydrated and avoid alcohol and strenuous activity during the first few days at high altitude.

If symptoms of altitude sickness appear, the most effective treatment is to descend to a lower elevation. Even a descent of a few hundred meters can significantly improve symptoms. Rest and hydration are also important. In severe cases, immediate descent and medical attention are critical.

Imagine climbing a high mountain pass and feeling a pounding headache and nausea. Recognizing the symptoms of altitude sickness, you decide to descend to a lower camp. After resting and hydrating, your symptoms improve, and you can safely continue your ascent with proper acclimatization.

Allergic Reactions

Allergic reactions can be triggered by insect stings, plants, food, or other environmental factors. Symptoms range from mild itching and swelling to severe anaphylaxis, which can be life-threatening.

For mild reactions, antihistamines can help reduce symptoms. Apply cool compresses to the affected area to relieve itching and swelling. If you know you have severe allergies, always carry an epinephrine auto-injector (EpiPen) and ensure that those traveling with you know how to use it.

In the event of a severe allergic reaction, administer epinephrine immediately and seek emergency medical help. Time is critical in such situations, and knowing how to respond quickly can save a life.

Imagine hiking through a field and suddenly feeling your skin itch and swell after brushing against a plant. You take an antihistamine from your first aid kit and apply a cool compress, finding relief from the discomfort. Your preparation and knowledge allow you to manage the reaction effectively.

General Principles of Managing Illness

In any illness scenario, the general principles of first aid apply: stay calm, assess the situation, and use your resources effectively. Ensure that your first aid kit is well-stocked with medications, bandages, and tools necessary for treating common illnesses. Know how to use each item and keep your kit easily accessible.

Always monitor symptoms closely and be prepared to make decisions based on the severity of the illness. If you're in a group, communicate clearly and ensure that everyone knows how to assist in case of an emergency. Preventing illness through good hygiene, proper hydration, and acclimatization is always better than treating it. Imagine leading a group through the wilderness and encountering an illness. You stay calm, assess the situation, and use your first aid skills to manage the symptoms. Your leadership and preparedness ensure that the group remains safe and healthy, allowing the adventure to continue.

1.3 EMERGENCY RESPONSE TECHNIQUES

Emergencies in the wilderness require swift and decisive action, often under challenging conditions. Whether dealing with severe injuries, sudden illnesses, or environmental hazards, knowing how to respond effectively can mean the difference between life and death. This chapter explores essential emergency response techniques, equipping you with the skills to handle critical situations with confidence and composure.

Assessing the Situation

The first step in any emergency response is to assess the situation calmly and thoroughly. Take a moment to breathe deeply and focus your thoughts. Scan the area for potential dangers that could further complicate the situation, such as unstable terrain, falling rocks, or aggressive wildlife.

Approach the injured person carefully, asking them to stay still if they're conscious and able to respond. Quickly determine the nature and extent of their injuries. This initial assessment helps prioritize your actions and resources.

Imagine approaching a fallen hiker who is conscious but in obvious pain. You notice a clear break in their leg and check for additional injuries. Ensuring the area is safe from further hazards, you begin to address the immediate needs.

Stabilizing Injuries

For serious injuries such as fractures, head wounds, or severe bleeding, stabilizing the injury is crucial. If a bone is broken, immobilize the limb using splints fashioned from branches, trekking poles, or other available materials. Pad the splints with clothing or fabric to avoid pressure sores and secure them with bandages or strips of cloth. If there is severe bleeding, apply direct pressure to the wound with a clean cloth or bandage. Elevate the injured area above heart level to reduce blood flow and wrap the wound securely. In the case of head injuries, keep the person still and monitor for signs of concussion, such as confusion, dizziness, or loss of consciousness. Imagine crafting a splint from sturdy branches and securing it around the broken leg. You carefully pad the splints with a shirt, ensuring they are snug but not too tight. The injured person's leg is now immobilized, reducing pain and preventing further damage.

Managing Shock

Shock is a common and potentially life-threatening response to severe injury or trauma. Symptoms include pale, clammy skin, rapid breathing, and a weak pulse. If untreated, shock can lead to unconsciousness and organ failure.

To manage shock, lay the person down on their back and elevate their legs about 12 inches to improve blood flow to vital organs. Keep them warm using blankets, sleeping bags, or spare clothing. Encourage them to stay calm and still, and reassure them that help is on the way. Monitor their vital signs regularly and be prepared to administer CPR if necessary.

Imagine comforting an injured hiker showing signs of shock. You lay them down, elevate their legs, and cover them with a blanket. Speaking calmly, you reassure them that help is coming, keeping their spirits up and their body warm.

Calling for Help

Effective communication is vital in an emergency. If you have access to a phone or satellite device, call emergency services immediately, providing clear and concise information about your location, the nature of the injury, and the condition of the injured person.

If you're out of communication range, you may need to send a member of your group to find help. Ensure they have clear instructions and know your exact location. Provide them with a map, compass, and any necessary identification details about the injured person.

Imagine using a satellite phone to call for help, describing your coordinates and the severity of the situation. You give detailed instructions to a fellow hiker who will go for help, ensuring they have all the necessary information to guide rescuers to your location.

Building a Shelter

In situations where immediate evacuation isn't possible, building a temporary shelter can protect the injured person from the elements and provide a safe place to wait for help. Use available materials like branches, leaves, and tarps to create a windproof and waterproof structure.

Keep the injured person comfortable by providing insulation from the ground using pine boughs, sleeping pads, or backpacks. Maintain their body temperature by using sleeping bags, blankets, or additional clothing. Ensure the shelter is visible to rescuers by marking it with brightly colored fabric or using a signal fire if safe to do so.

Imagine constructing a lean-to shelter with branches and a tarp, securing it against a sturdy tree. You lay out a sleeping pad and cover the injured person with a sleeping bag, making them as comfortable as possible while waiting for help.

Administering CPR

In cases where the injured person is unresponsive and not breathing, administering CPR can be a lifesaving measure. Begin by checking for responsiveness by tapping their shoulder and shouting their name. If there is no response, call for help and begin CPR.

Place the heel of your hand on the center of their chest, interlocking your fingers. Perform chest compressions at a rate of 100 to 120 per minute, pressing down about 2 inches deep. After 30 compressions, give two rescue breaths by tilting their head back, lifting their chin, and breathing into their mouth.

Continue CPR until help arrives or the person regains consciousness. If an automated external defibrillator (AED) is available, use it as directed.

Imagine finding an unresponsive hiker. You immediately begin CPR, performing chest compressions and rescue breaths with precision. Your training and quick response keep the blood flowing, providing a critical lifeline until professional help can take over.

Monitoring and Reassuring

While waiting for help to arrive, continuously monitor the injured person's condition. Check their vital signs regularly, including pulse, breathing, and consciousness. Offer reassurance and keep them informed about what you're doing and why.

This helps reduce anxiety and keeps their spirits up. Maintain a calm and positive demeanor, as your attitude can significantly impact the injured person's mental state. Keep them engaged by talking about familiar, comforting topics or guiding them through deep breathing exercises to manage pain and anxiety. Imagine sitting next to the injured hiker, holding their hand and speaking softly about your shared love of the outdoors. You monitor their pulse and breathing, ensuring they feel cared for and supported while waiting for rescuers.

2. Natural Remedies

2.1 Medicinal Plants and Their Uses

Yarrow (Achillea millefolium)

Yarrow, with its feathery leaves and clusters of white or pink flowers, is a versatile medicinal plant found in many regions. Known for its ability to stop bleeding, yarrow can be a vital resource for treating wounds in the wild.

To use yarrow, crush the fresh leaves and flowers to release their juices, then apply them directly to cuts or abrasions. This application helps to staunch bleeding and promote healing. Yarrow can also be made into a poultice by mixing the crushed plant with a small amount of water and applying it to the wound.

Imagine you've cut your hand while setting up camp. You find a patch of yarrow nearby, crush the leaves, and press them onto the cut. Within moments, the bleeding slows, and you feel a sense of relief knowing that nature has provided a remedy.

Plantain (Plantago major and Plantago lanceolata)

Plantain, often considered a common weed, is a powerful medicinal plant with broad applications. Its leaves contain anti-inflammatory and antimicrobial properties, making it excellent for treating insect bites, stings, and minor wounds.

To use plantain, chew or crush the leaves to create a moist pulp, then apply it to the affected area. This action draws out toxins and soothes the skin. For more substantial relief, plantain leaves can be made into a salve or tea.

Imagine being bitten by a mosquito. The itch is persistent and distracting. You spot some plantain growing nearby, chew a leaf to release its juices, and apply it to the bite. Almost instantly, the itching subsides, and you continue your hike with renewed comfort.

Echinacea (Echinacea purpurea)

Echinacea, with its distinctive purple petals, is widely recognized for its immune-boosting properties. It can be a crucial ally in preventing and treating colds and other infections in the wilderness.

To utilize echinacea, the roots and leaves can be brewed into a tea. This tea helps stimulate the immune system, reducing the severity and duration of symptoms. Fresh echinacea can also be chewed or used as a tincture.

Imagine feeling the onset of a cold while camping in the mountains. You prepare a tea using echinacea leaves and roots, sipping it slowly as you rest. The warmth and medicinal properties of the tea bolster your immune system, helping you fend off the illness.

Willow (Salix spp.)

Willow trees, commonly found near water sources, provide a natural source of salicylic acid, the active ingredient in aspirin. This makes willow bark an effective pain reliever and anti-inflammatory agent.

To use willow bark, strip a small amount of bark from a young branch and boil it to make a tea. Drinking this tea can alleviate headaches, muscle pain, and fever. Imagine a long day of trekking leaving you with aching muscles. You gather some willow bark, boil it, and drink the tea. The natural salicylic acid eases your pain, allowing you to rest comfortably and prepare for the next day's journey.

Aloe Vera (Aloe barbadensis miller)

Aloe vera is a well-known plant for treating burns, cuts, and skin irritations. Its succulent leaves contain a gel that provides soothing relief and accelerates healing. To use aloe vera, cut a leaf and apply the gel directly to the affected area. This application cools burns, reduces inflammation, and promotes skin regeneration.

Imagine accidentally burning your hand while cooking over a campfire. You find an aloe vera plant, cut a leaf, and apply the gel to the burn. The immediate cooling sensation provides relief, and you know the aloe will help the skin heal faster.

Elderberry (Sambucus nigra)

Elderberry is a potent antiviral and immune-boosting plant. Its dark berries can be used to make syrups and teas that help combat colds and flu. To use elderberries, cook them to make a syrup or brew them into a tea.

This preparation helps alleviate respiratory symptoms and strengthen the immune response.

Imagine feeling the first signs of a sore throat and congestion. You prepare a tea with elderberries, sipping it slowly as you rest. The antiviral properties of the elderberries provide comfort and support your body in fighting off the illness.

Chamomile (Matricaria chamomilla)

Chamomile is renowned for its calming effects and can be used to treat anxiety, insomnia, and digestive issues. Its small, daisy-like flowers are a gentle yet effective remedy.

To use chamomile, brew the flowers into a tea. Drinking this tea before bed can help soothe the mind and promote restful sleep. It can also relieve stomach cramps and indigestion.

Imagine a restless night in the wilderness, your mind racing with thoughts of the day's adventures. You brew a cup of chamomile tea, its soothing warmth helping to calm your mind and ease you into a peaceful sleep.

2.2 PREPARING HERBAL TREATMENTS

The first step in preparing herbal treatments is correctly identifying and harvesting the right plants. Accurate identification is crucial, as some plants can be harmful if misused. Familiarize yourself with the appearance, habitat, and key characteristics of medicinal plants. Carry a reliable field guide to assist with identification.

Harvest plants sustainably, taking only what you need and ensuring that the plant population remains healthy. Early morning is often the best time to gather herbs, as the plants are fresh and full of dew. Use a sharp knife or scissors to harvest, minimizing damage to the plant.

Imagine walking through a sunlit meadow, a field guide in hand. You spot a cluster of echinacea, their purple petals vibrant against the green backdrop. Carefully, you harvest a few leaves and roots, ensuring to leave enough behind for the plant to thrive.

Drying Herbs

Drying herbs preserves their medicinal properties and extends their shelf life. To dry herbs, spread them out in a single layer on a clean, dry surface away from direct sunlight. Good air circulation is essential to prevent mold growth. Alternatively, bundle the herbs and hang them upside down in a dry, well-ventilated area.

The drying process can take several days to weeks, depending on the plant and environmental conditions. Once dried, store the herbs in airtight containers, away from light and moisture.

Imagine hanging bundles of sage and mint in a shaded corner of your camp. Over the next few days, you watch as the leaves gradually dry and curl, their aromatic oils concentrating. You feel a sense of accomplishment, knowing these herbs are ready to be used when needed.

Making Herbal Teas

Herbal teas, or infusions, are one of the simplest and most effective ways to use medicinal plants. To make an herbal tea, boil water and pour it over the dried or fresh herbs. Cover and steep for 10-20 minutes, allowing the beneficial compounds to infuse into the water.

The type and amount of herb used can vary based on the desired effect. Common herbal teas include chamomile for relaxation, peppermint for digestion, and elderberry for immune support.

Imagine a chilly evening by the campfire, the sky darkening as you prepare a pot of elderberry tea. You pour the hot water over the dried berries, inhaling the fragrant steam. As you sip the warm, comforting tea, you feel the soothing effects take hold, warding off the chill and boosting your immune system.

Creating Tinctures

Tinctures are concentrated herbal extracts made by soaking herbs in alcohol or vinegar. They are potent, long-lasting, and easy to carry. To make a tincture, fill a jar with chopped fresh or dried herbs, then cover them with alcohol, such as vodka or brandy, or apple cider vinegar. Seal the jar and store it in a dark, cool place for several weeks, shaking it daily.

After about six weeks, strain the liquid through a fine mesh or cheesecloth into a clean bottle. This liquid is your tincture, a powerful remedy that can be taken by the dropperful.

Imagine preparing a tincture of echinacea. You fill a jar with the fresh plant material and cover it with vodka. Over the next few weeks, you shake the jar daily, watching as the liquid darkens and absorbs the herb's properties. Finally, you strain the tincture, feeling a sense of pride as you bottle the potent extract.

Making Salves and Ointments

Salves and ointments are ideal for topical applications, such as treating cuts, burns, and rashes. They are made by infusing herbs in oil and then thickening the mixture with beeswax. To make a salve, heat a carrier oil (like olive or coconut oil) and add dried herbs.

Simmer on low heat for several hours, allowing the herbs to infuse their healing properties into the oil. Strain the mixture, then reheat gently and add beeswax until the desired consistency is achieved. Pour the salve into small jars or tins to cool and solidify.

Imagine crafting a healing salve from yarrow and calendula. You infuse the herbs in coconut oil, the warm aroma filling the air. After straining the mixture, you add beeswax and pour the golden liquid into small tins. As the salve cools and solidifies, you know you have a powerful remedy ready to soothe wounds and irritations.

Preparing Poultices

Poultices are another effective way to use herbs for external treatment. A poultice involves crushing fresh or dried herbs and applying them directly to the skin. This method is excellent for drawing out infections, reducing inflammation, and soothing pain.

To make a poultice, chop the herbs finely and mix with a small amount of hot water to form a paste. Spread the paste on a clean cloth or directly on the skin, then cover with another cloth to hold it in place. Leave the poultice on for 20-30 minutes, allowing the herbs to work their magic.

Imagine treating a sprained ankle with a comfrey poultice. You crush the fresh comfrey leaves, mix them with hot water, and apply the paste to the swollen area. Wrapping it with a cloth, you feel the soothing effect of the herb reducing the inflammation and pain.

Crafting Herbal Oils

Herbal oils are used for massage, skincare, and healing. To make an herbal oil, infuse dried herbs in a carrier oil over several weeks. This process extracts the medicinal properties of the herbs into the oil.

Fill a jar with dried herbs and cover with a carrier oil. Seal the jar and place it in a warm, sunny spot for 2-3 weeks, shaking it daily. After the infusion period, strain the oil and store it in a dark bottle.

Imagine creating a lavender oil for soothing massages. You fill a jar with dried lavender flowers and cover them with olive oil. Over the next few weeks, you watch as the sun warms the jar, infusing the oil with the calming scent of lavender. Once strained, the oil is ready to provide relaxation and relief.

2.3 PREVENTATIVE HEALTH MEASURES

Preventative health measures are the cornerstone of well-being, especially when you're venturing into the wilderness. By adopting a proactive approach to health, you can prevent many common ailments and ensure that you remain strong and resilient throughout your journey. This chapter explores various preventative health strategies, highlighting how natural remedies can support and enhance these practices.

Imagine setting out on a multi-day trek through rugged mountains and dense forests. The excitement of adventure is matched by the awareness that maintaining your health is crucial for a successful trip. Preventative measures are your first line of defense, safeguarding you against potential health issues before they arise.

Boosting Immunity

A strong immune system is your best ally in the wilderness. It helps fend off infections and keeps your body functioning optimally. Several natural remedies can bolster your immune defenses, ensuring you stay healthy in challenging conditions.

Echinacea, known for its immune-boosting properties, can be taken as a tea or tincture before and during your trip. Regular consumption of this herb stimulates your body's defenses, making you less susceptible to colds and infections.

Imagine sipping a warm cup of echinacea tea each morning as you prepare for the day's hike. The earthy flavor reminds you of the plant's protective benefits, giving you confidence that your immune system is ready to handle the rigors of the trail.

Hydration and Nutrition

Proper hydration and nutrition are fundamental to maintaining health. Dehydration and poor diet can lead to fatigue, illness, and impaired physical performance. Drinking plenty of water and consuming a balanced diet rich in vitamins and minerals are essential.

Herbal teas, such as nettle and peppermint, not only provide hydration but also offer a range of nutrients. Nettle tea, for example, is packed with vitamins A and C, iron, and calcium, supporting overall health and energy levels. Peppermint tea aids digestion and keeps your body hydrated.

Imagine a midday break by a clear mountain stream. You refill your water bottle and brew a cup of nettle tea, savoring its refreshing taste. The tea not only quenches your thirst but also delivers vital nutrients, keeping you energized and ready for the next leg of your journey.

Skin Protection

Protecting your skin from the elements is crucial in the wilderness. Sunburn, insect bites, and abrasions can all lead to discomfort and health issues. Natural remedies offer effective protection and treatment for these common problems.

Aloe vera is a versatile plant that soothes sunburn and promotes skin healing. Apply the gel from an aloe vera leaf directly to sunburned skin for instant relief. For insect bites, a plantain poultice can reduce itching and inflammation. Simply crush the leaves and apply them to the affected area.

Imagine a long day of hiking under the hot sun. In the evening, you apply aloe vera gel to your sunburned arms, feeling the cooling relief spread over your skin. Later, when a mosquito bite starts to itch, you crush some plantain leaves and place them on the bite, the irritation quickly subsiding.

Mental Health and Stress Management

Maintaining mental health is just as important as physical health. The wilderness can be both exhilarating and stressful, so it's essential to have strategies in place for managing stress and staying mentally balanced.

Adaptogenic herbs like ashwagandha and rhodiola can help your body adapt to stress and maintain mental clarity. These herbs can be taken as supplements or brewed into teas. Additionally, practices such as mindfulness and meditation, supported by the tranquil natural environment, can significantly enhance your mental well-being.

Imagine sitting quietly by a serene lake, the surface reflecting the surrounding trees. You take a few moments to practice deep breathing and mindfulness, grounding yourself in the present moment. A cup of rhodiola tea in hand, you feel the calming effects of the herb, helping you to remain centered and focused.

Hygiene Practices

Good hygiene is vital in preventing infections and illnesses. Simple practices such as regular handwashing, dental care, and proper food handling can prevent a host of problems.

Carrying a small bottle of tea tree oil can be incredibly useful. Known for its antiseptic properties, tea tree oil can be used to clean minor cuts and scrapes, keeping them free from infection. Adding a few drops to your handwashing routine enhances its effectiveness.

Imagine setting up camp for the night and using a few drops of tea tree oil in your water for washing your hands and face. The refreshing scent and antiseptic properties give you peace of mind, knowing you're maintaining good hygiene even in the wild.

Adequate Rest and Sleep

Rest and sleep are crucial for recovery and overall health. A well-rested body is better equipped to handle the physical and mental demands of wilderness travel.

Herbs like chamomile and valerian root can aid in achieving restful sleep. Drinking a cup of chamomile tea before bed helps relax your muscles and mind, preparing you for a night of deep, restorative sleep. Valerian root can be used similarly to reduce anxiety and promote relaxation.

Imagine lying in your tent, the sounds of nature creating a peaceful backdrop. You sip on chamomile tea, feeling your body unwind. As you drift off to sleep, you know you're giving your body the rest it needs to tackle the adventures of the coming day.

Preventing Common Ailments

Preventative measures also include guarding against common ailments like respiratory infections and digestive issues. Herbs like elderberry and ginger are excellent for these purposes.

Elderberry syrup can be taken daily to ward off respiratory infections. Its antiviral properties help keep colds and flu at bay. Ginger, on the other hand, is great for digestion. A ginger tea can soothe an upset stomach and improve digestion, preventing discomfort during your travels.

Imagine starting each day with a spoonful of elderberry syrup, a simple routine that boosts your immunity.

Later, after a hearty camp meal, you brew a ginger tea, its spicy warmth settling your stomach and ensuring you feel comfortable and ready for the journey ahead.

3. Mental Health and Group Dynamics

3.1 Coping with Isolation and Stress

Solitude in the wilderness offers a unique opportunity for self-reflection and personal growth. Embrace this time as a chance to reconnect with yourself and the natural world. Mindfulness practices, such as meditation and deep breathing, can help center your thoughts and reduce anxiety.

Find a quiet spot, sit comfortably, and focus on your breath. Inhale deeply through your nose, hold for a few seconds, and exhale slowly through your mouth. As you breathe, let your surroundings ground you. Listen to the wind rustling through the trees, the distant call of a bird, or the gentle flow of a stream. These sounds become your anchor, bringing you back to the present moment.

Imagine sitting by a serene lake at sunrise, the sky painted in hues of pink and orange. You close your eyes and breathe deeply, each inhale filling your lungs with fresh air, each exhale releasing tension. The tranquility of the scene around you seeps into your being, easing your mind and calming your spirit.

Maintaining Routine and Structure

Creating a daily routine provides a sense of normalcy and control, which is particularly comforting in an unpredictable environment. Establish a schedule that includes activities such as setting up camp, preparing meals, and exploring your surroundings. This structure not only keeps you productive but also helps mitigate feelings of aimlessness and anxiety.

Break your day into manageable segments, setting small goals to achieve throughout. For instance, dedicate the morning to hiking, the afternoon to setting up camp and foraging, and the evening to relaxing and reflecting. Each task, no matter how small, becomes a milestone that fosters a sense of accomplishment and purpose.

Imagine waking up at dawn, the air crisp and cool. You follow your routine: packing up your gear, making a hearty breakfast, and plotting the day's route on your map. As the sun rises higher, you feel a sense of readiness and determination, each step in your routine reinforcing your resolve.

Staying Connected

Even in isolation, it's important to maintain connections with loved ones. Modern technology, such as satellite phones and GPS devices, allows for periodic communication with the outside world. Sending updates on your progress and receiving messages from family and friends can provide emotional support and reduce feelings of loneliness.

If technology is unavailable, consider keeping a journal. Write about your experiences, thoughts, and emotions. This practice not only serves as a mental outlet but also creates a record of your journey that you can share with others upon your return.

Imagine writing in your journal by the light of a campfire. The pages fill with descriptions of the landscapes you've traversed, the challenges you've faced, and the moments of joy and reflection. This act of writing bridges the gap between you and the outside world, capturing the essence of your adventure.

Practicing Self-Care

Self-care is essential for managing stress and maintaining mental health. Take time each day to engage in activities that nurture your well-being. This might include physical exercises such as yoga or stretching, which keep your body limber and reduce stress. Additionally, reading a favorite book or listening to music can provide comfort and relaxation.

Nutrition also plays a crucial role in mental health. Ensure that your diet includes a balance of carbohydrates, proteins, and fats to keep your energy levels stable. Carry herbal teas like chamomile or lavender, which have calming properties and can help soothe your mind after a long day.

Imagine ending your day with a few gentle yoga stretches, feeling your muscles relax and your mind unwind. You brew a cup of chamomile tea, the warm, soothing liquid helping to wash away the day's stresses. As you lie in your sleeping bag, you feel a deep sense of peace and readiness for the next day's challenges.

Fostering Resilience

Resilience is the ability to adapt and thrive despite adversity. Building resilience involves cultivating a positive mindset, learning from experiences, and maintaining a sense of hope. Reflect on past challenges you've overcome and remind yourself of your strengths and capabilities.

Positive self-talk can reinforce resilience. Replace negative thoughts with affirmations of your abilities and determination. Visualize successful outcomes and focus on the progress you've made rather than the difficulties ahead.

Imagine facing a steep, rocky ascent. The climb seems daunting, but you take a moment to remind yourself of the mountains you've conquered before. With each step, you repeat a mantra of strength and perseverance, visualizing yourself at the summit. This mental fortitude propels you forward, one step at a time.

Seeking Joy in Small Moments

In the wilderness, joy can be found in the simplest of moments. Watching a sunset, hearing the call of an owl, or finding a particularly beautiful leaf can bring profound happiness. Cultivate a sense of gratitude for these small wonders, allowing them to uplift your spirit.

Keep your senses open to the beauty around you. Touch the rough bark of a tree, smell the earth after a rain, taste the freshness of a wild berry. These sensory experiences ground you in the present and remind you of the magic inherent in nature.

Imagine sitting quietly on a hill, watching the sun dip below the horizon. The sky is ablaze with colors, and a sense of peace washes over you. This moment of pure beauty fills you with gratitude and joy, a powerful antidote to the stresses of the day.

3.2 Group Leadership and Morale

Leading a group in the wilderness is both a privilege and a responsibility. Effective leadership and maintaining high morale are crucial for the success of any outdoor adventure. When group dynamics are positive and well-managed, the journey becomes not only safer but also more enjoyable and rewarding for everyone involved. This sub-chapter explores the art of group leadership and the strategies to foster strong morale, ensuring a harmonious and resilient team.

The tone of the expedition is set from the very beginning. As a leader, your attitude, enthusiasm, and approachability create the foundation for group morale. Greet each member with a warm smile and a few encouraging words. Establish an atmosphere of openness and mutual respect, where everyone feels valued and heard. From the outset, communicate the goals and expectations clearly.

Explain the itinerary, highlight key milestones, and outline the roles and responsibilities of each member. This clarity helps to align everyone's efforts and fosters a sense of shared purpose. Imagine gathering your group around at the start, the excitement palpable. You speak with confidence and warmth, outlining the day's plan and inviting everyone to share their thoughts and expectations. This initial interaction sets a positive tone, encouraging open communication and collaboration. Involving everyone in decision-making processes and daily tasks strengthens group cohesion and morale. Encourage each member to contribute their ideas and skills, fostering a sense of ownership and investment in the journey. Whether it's choosing the next campsite, cooking meals, or navigating a tricky section of the trail, collaborative efforts build trust and camaraderie.

Recognize and utilize the unique strengths of each member. Someone might be a great navigator, another an excellent cook, and someone else a natural storyteller who can lift spirits around the campfire. By appreciating and leveraging these diverse talents, you enhance the group's overall effectiveness and enjoyment.

Imagine a moment when the trail forks, and the group needs to decide which path to take. You invite everyone to share their insights and preferences, leading a thoughtful discussion. The final decision is a collective one, and the sense of unity is strengthened as you all move forward together.

Conflict is an inevitable part of any group dynamic, especially in the demanding environment of the wilderness. Addressing issues promptly and fairly is essential to maintaining morale. Approach conflicts with empathy and a focus on resolution rather than blame. Encourage open dialogue, where each person can express their perspective in a respectful and constructive manner.

Sometimes, the challenges will be external, such as harsh weather or difficult terrain. In these moments, your ability to remain calm and decisive is crucial. Lead by example, showing resilience and adaptability. Reassure your group, reminding them of their strengths and the progress they've made.

Imagine a sudden storm forcing an unplanned detour. The group is tired and tensions rise. You gather everyone, acknowledge the challenges, and reaffirm your confidence in their abilities. Together, you devise a new plan, transforming a moment of adversity into one of teamwork and determination. Recognition and celebration of achievements, no matter how small, boost morale and foster a positive group dynamic.

Take the time to acknowledge individual contributions and collective accomplishments. Whether it's reaching a significant waypoint, overcoming a tough climb, or simply maintaining a positive attitude, celebrate these moments.

Incorporate rituals or small ceremonies to mark these milestones. A shared meal, a few words of appreciation, or a group photo can make these moments memorable. These celebrations not only lift spirits but also strengthen the bonds within the group. Imagine reaching a stunning mountain vista after a challenging ascent. You pause to let everyone catch their breath and then gather the group for a heartfelt acknowledgment of their efforts. A group photo captures the moment, and you share a special treat to celebrate the achievement, solidifying the sense of unity and accomplishment.

A leader's responsibility extends to the physical and mental well-being of the group. Monitor the health of each member, watching for signs of fatigue, injury, or stress. Encourage regular breaks, proper hydration, and nutritious meals. Be attentive to the emotional state of your team, offering support and encouragement when needed. Promote activities that enhance mental well-being, such as mindfulness exercises, storytelling, or simply appreciating the beauty of the surroundings. Create an environment where it's okay to express vulnerability and seek help. This support network is vital for maintaining morale and fostering a resilient group.

Imagine noticing a team member who seems unusually quiet and withdrawn. You take a moment to walk with them, offering a listening ear and words of encouragement. This small act of kindness helps to lift their spirits and reinforces the supportive culture of the group. Ultimately, the most powerful tool for a leader is their own behavior. Leading by example, you demonstrate the values and attitudes you wish to see in your group. Show respect, patience, and enthusiasm. Approach challenges with a positive mindset and a willingness to find solutions. Your actions speak louder than words. When you maintain a calm demeanor in the face of adversity, exhibit genuine care for each member, and uphold the principles of fairness and respect, you inspire your group to do the same.

3.3 CONFLICT RESOLUTION SKILLS

Conflict is an inevitable part of any group dynamic, especially in the challenging and unpredictable environment of the wilderness. Learning to navigate and resolve conflicts effectively is crucial for maintaining group harmony, ensuring safety, and fostering a positive and productive atmosphere.

Conflicts often arise from misunderstandings, unmet needs, or differing perspectives. In the wilderness, stress, exhaustion, and the high stakes of survival can amplify these issues. The first step in conflict resolution is to understand the underlying causes. Is the disagreement about a specific decision, or is it rooted in deeper issues like personality clashes or unspoken grievances?

Take the time to listen actively to each party involved. Encourage them to express their feelings and concerns openly. This not only helps you understand the situation better but also makes the individuals feel heard and valued.

Imagine two group members arguing over the route to take. You take them aside, listen to their viewpoints, and realize that one is worried about safety while the other is concerned about time. By acknowledging these underlying concerns, you can address the real issues rather than just the surface disagreement.

A safe and respectful environment is essential for productive conflict resolution. Ensure that all parties feel comfortable expressing themselves without fear of judgment or retribution. Establish ground rules for the discussion, such as speaking one at a time, avoiding personal attacks, and focusing on solutions rather than blame. Facilitate the conversation with a neutral and calm demeanor. Your role is to guide the dialogue constructively, helping each person articulate their perspective clearly and respectfully.

Imagine gathering the group in a circle, setting the tone with a calm and neutral stance. You remind everyone of the importance of respect and listening, creating an atmosphere where open dialogue can occur.

Empathy and active listening are powerful tools in conflict resolution. Show empathy by acknowledging the emotions and viewpoints of each party. Use reflective listening techniques, such as summarizing what you've heard and asking clarifying questions, to ensure you fully understand their perspective. This approach not only helps de-escalate tensions but also fosters mutual respect and understanding.

When individuals feel genuinely heard, they are more likely to move towards compromise and resolution.

Imagine actively listening to a frustrated group member, reflecting their feelings back to them: "I hear that you're concerned about the steepness of the trail and the safety risks involved." This validation helps lower their defenses and opens the door to finding a shared solution.

In the wilderness, the ultimate goal is the safety and well-being of the group. Highlighting these common objectives can help reframe the conflict and remind everyone of their shared purpose. Encourage the group to focus on what unites them rather than what divides them.

Identify common goals and use them as a foundation for finding solutions. This approach shifts the focus from individual differences to collective success.

Imagine reminding the group of their shared goal: "We all want to reach the campsite safely and enjoy this journey together." By refocusing on this common aim, you create a collaborative mindset that makes finding a resolution easier.

Encourage a collaborative approach to problem-solving. Invite each party to suggest solutions and work together to find a mutually acceptable outcome. This inclusive process empowers everyone involved and increases their commitment to the resolution.

Facilitate brainstorming sessions where all ideas are considered without judgment. Once all options are on the table, evaluate them collectively, considering the pros and cons of each.

Imagine facilitating a brainstorming session where everyone suggests potential routes and strategies. You guide the discussion, helping the group weigh the safety and time factors until they arrive at a consensus that satisfies both sides.

Compromise is often necessary to resolve conflicts. Encourage all parties to be flexible and open to finding middle ground. Sometimes, this means each person has to give up something for the greater good of the group. Emphasize the importance of adaptability and the willingness to adjust plans as needed. In the wilderness, flexibility can be the key to survival and success. Imagine both parties agreeing to a route that is slightly longer but safer, finding a compromise that addresses the primary concerns of both sides.

This willingness to adjust plans for the collective good strengthens group unity. Once a resolution is reached, focus on moving forward positively. Reinforce the group's cohesion by acknowledging the effort it took to resolve the conflict and celebrating the successful outcome.

Encourage a sense of closure by ensuring that any lingering feelings of resentment or misunderstanding are addressed. Foster an environment where lessons learned from the conflict are viewed as opportunities for growth and improved teamwork. Imagine concluding the discussion with a positive note: "I'm proud of how we worked through this together. Let's continue supporting each other and make the rest of this journey even better." This affirmation helps to heal any residual tensions and strengthens group morale. Conflict resolution skills can be honed and developed over time. Encourage your group to practice these skills regularly, both in and out of conflict situations. Role-playing scenarios, reflective discussions, and feedback sessions can all contribute to building a more resilient and harmonious group dynamic. Imagine leading a reflective discussion around the campfire, where the group shares insights and feedback on how the conflict was handled. This continuous learning process enhances everyone's skills and prepares them for future challenges.

Made in the USA
Coppell, TX
27 June 2024

34015573R00116